Voices of Hope

Stick Your Neck Out

Giraffe Heroes Project

At a staff meeting of the Giraffe Heroes Project one fine spring morning, President John Graham announced that he had something to show us all and began doodling a book outline on a flip chart. It was called *Voices of Hope*. He'd seen the whole concept in a dream and soon had all of us seeing what he saw—a book of readings from our storybank of Giraffe Heroes, inspiring people to read *and* to move into service themselves. Within an hour we had the cover done. By the end of the day, we'd found a literacy expert to advise us and had started the work of gathering the stories and photos. We didn't have the funding to create a new book, but we all shared this powerful vision, so we stuck our necks out—we knew we'd find the funding. And we did. This book is the result of that shared vision. Believe in your visions. Stick your neck out.

—*The Giraffe Staff*

Funding for the creation and distribution of *Voices of Hope* has been provided by~

The Virginia Wellington Cabot Foundation
The May and Stanley Smith Charitable Trust
The Lucky Seven Foundation
Costco
Jacqueline Merrill
The Roy A. Hunt Foundation
&
Supporters of the Giraffe Heroes Project

Voices of Hope
Heroes' Stories
For Challenging Times

Readings from
the Giraffe Heroes Project

Voices of Hope, Second Edition

Published by the Giraffe Heroes Project
PO Box 759
Langley WA 98260
office@giraffe.org
www.giraffe.org

Project manager: John Graham
Stories: From the archives of the Giraffe Heroes Project
Principal writers: Ann Medlock, Keith Mack, Lynn Willeford, Chris
    Douthitt, Marian Blue and Leslye Wood
Editor: Ann Medlock
Copyeditors: Mary Ella Keblusek and Sue Keblusek
Reviewers: Karyn Watkins and Maggie Bedrosian
Designer: Susan Reed, *www.pixelsgraphics.com*
Production manager: Mary Ella Keblusek

Manufactured in the United States of America
Printed on recycled paper

ISBN 1-893805-07-07

1 2 3 4 5   07 06 05

Also from the Giraffe Heroes Project

You can go to *www.giraffe.org* to order –

A teacher's guide to this book

The K-12 Giraffe Heroes Program – A full curriculum for character education and service learning in grades K-2, 3-5, 6-9, and 10-12

It's Up To Us – A handbook for teens on moving into courageous service

101 Giraffe Heroes – Scripts for reading out loud, each telling a Giraffe Hero's story

www.giraffe.org – A Web site full of stories, ideas and news about Giraffe Heroes

Stan & Bea's *Two Tall Tales* – Audio stories for children about how the giraffe got its long neck

A ten-minute DVD on the history of the Giraffe Heroes Project

Stick Your Neck Out: A Street-smart Guide to Creating Change in Your Community and Beyond

Posters, T-shirts, pens and mugs, all featuring the big red giraffe and all available at *www.giraffe.org*

Table of Contents

Dear Reader,

The book you're holding comes to you from the Giraffe Heroes Project, a group whose job is to honor people who stick their necks out for the common good. We've been telling these heroes' stories in the media and in schools for a long time.

Now we've put together 40 of our stories and put them in your hands, as reading materials. That's this book, *Voices of Hope*.

You'll find this isn't like other books of readings for students—some of those books seem so intent on improving your reading skills that they forget the material should be *interesting*, or why should you *want* to read it? The people you'll meet by reading this book—and the stories of what they've done—are, to say the least, interesting. Maybe "fascinating" would be more accurate.

That's the way it's always been. Since the beginning of time, humans have told each other heroes' stories and we've always loved hearing them. Real heroes show us the very best that's possible for people to achieve, and they help us believe in our own capacity to be brave and caring.

Throughout this book, you'll find questions and ideas that will indeed help you build your reading skills, but you'll also find ideas for things to do in the world, just as these heroes have done.

If or when you read about a Giraffe Hero who's taken action on a problem that concerns you, or if one of their stories sets you thinking about some other problem, follow that train of thought. As you can see from many of the stories in this book, you don't have to be 21 or have some special degrees before you can be a brave and caring citizen. Anyone who gets involved in making the community a better place is one of its valuable citizens.

You may not know exactly what to do, but your teacher has a guide to this course that outlines exactly how to proceed, starting from a concern you might have, all the way to completing a project that addresses that concern.

So as you read, keep thinking of the things you care about, and know that you *can* do something that will help, just as all these Giraffe Heroes have done.

There are even more Giraffe Heroes at *www.giraffe.org*. And if you've got a little brother or sister, try the Kids Only section of that website for stories they'll enjoy too.

OK, some specifics about using this book. First of all we want you to enjoy meeting the people on these pages. Read each story and see what feelings it brings up for you. Imagine *being* the

> Since the beginning of time, humans have told each other heroes' stories...

person you're reading about. How did it feel to be in that person's situation? *Be* there with each of them.

After you've really taken in the story, there's time to do the details, like figuring out any words that are new or unfamiliar. When you get to the Vocabulary part of the To Do section of each and every story, repeat this exercise:

> **Find any words in this story that are not completely familiar to you. See if you can understand their meanings by the way they're used in the story. Then look them up in a dictionary and put them in the *journal* you're keeping for this course, with a brief definition of each one. Use each word in a sentence that you make up yourself.**

We didn't put that paragraph after each story—it would be boring to read it over and over. But don't forget to *do* it—over and over.

By the end of the book, you should have hundreds of new words in that journal, ready to use any time you might need them. The journal will also hold all your thoughts on what you read here.

While you're at it, make sure you've got the spellings down. You may think an almost-right spelling of a word is OK. It's not. Misspelled words are a fine way to make your reader lose confidence that your words are worth reading. I know that's harsh, but trust me, in the world of work and of normal communications with adults, spelling *counts*.

Some people, myself among them, love playing with words. Don't be afraid to fool around with a Thesaurus—that's where you'll find all the words you might use *instead* of the one you're adding to your journal. Try making up words that never existed but could be useful. (Shakespeare did that all the time—why not you? He wrote that one of his characters "spanieled" after a woman. To "spaniel" is not really a word. But you can get it, right? The character followed that woman around as if he were her pet dog.)

It's amazing what you can find out by just bouncing around in a dictionary.

When you look up words in the dictionary, see if there's anything else interesting on the page where your target word is. Say you're looking up "inorganic." What else is on the page? Hmmm. "Innocuous." That's a good one. And how about "innuendo"? It's amazing what you can find out by just bouncing around in a dictionary.

Even punctuation can be fun. If you don't believe me, check out the books *Eats, Shoots and Leaves* and *The New Well-Tempered Sentence; A Punctuation Handbook for the Innocent, the Eager, and the Doomed*. The authors can make you laugh as they play around with commas and question marks!

The second part of what's going on in this book is service-learning, a way to combine your classroom learning with real-world activities. Because this is from the Giraffe Heroes Project, our service-learning ideas are all about being active citizens in our democracy.

At the end of every lesson ask yourself if you're inspired to do something for others. If or when you are, your teacher has a guide to this course that can supply you with all the information you need to get from inspiration to completion of a successful service idea.

It should be *your* idea, something you care about and can commit to working on. Being told to go help at a homeless shelter isn't what this is about. We say it has to be your concern and your idea of how to make a difference. If that turns out to be helping at a homeless shelter, fine. Just so it's what you really care about and really want to do.

You can work with your whole class, if you all agree on something to do together. You can be on a small team. You can work in a pair or alone. It's up to you.

We just urge you to be sure that what you choose to do is a stretch for you. You don't have to take on a huge problem and work on it for the rest of your life. Just be sure you don't stop at what's easy and unchallenging for you. Whatever you think your limits are, go at least a little past them by doing something that involves learning new things, trying new skills, getting out beyond your comfort zone.

...be sure that what you choose to do is a stretch for you...

We call that sticking your neck out.

From all of us at the Giraffe Heroes Project, good luck on this journey.

— *Ann Medlock*
Founder

PS: Tell us what happens in your class! You can email the story to *office@giraffe.org* and it may turn up on our website as ideas for other kids. (And you'll check your spelling, won't you?)

Stick Your Neck Out

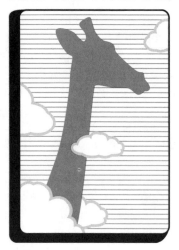

When You Really Need a Friend

When **Roxanne Black** was 15, she was diagnosed with lupus—a serious, chronic disease. She was devastated. She wanted to talk to someone who really understood what she was going through, someone her own age who also had lupus. She started searching for that person who would understand how she felt.

She didn't find that personal friend she was looking for, at least not right away, but she did find a whole new mission for her life—other people with serious illnesses were looking for someone who understood, just as Roxane was. They felt alone, especially those suffering from unusual illnesses.

Black formed the Friends' Health Connection, which she has built into a national support network for thousands of people with serious illnesses, injuries or disabilities. The Connection links them to someone with whom they can share information, while they keep each other's spirits up. She also organized a semi-annual auction that has raised thousands of dollars for lupus research and public education.

While in college, Black suffered a kidney failure, not unusual among people with lupus. Not one to waste time, she did computer work for Friends' Health Connection while undergoing five-times-a-day kidney dialysis treatments.

An organ transplant was necessary if she was to survive; her sister donated the needed kidney. After the operation, Black launched a campaign to get the word out that organ donations are down and that thousands of critically ill people need more of their fellow citizens to sign organ donor cards.

Friends' Health Connection has gone into dozens of hospitals, helping thousands of people connect with supportive new friends right from their hospital rooms, immediately after being diagnosed. Connection members are also given an array of information on health and well-being, via the Internet.

And six years after starting her search, Roxanne Black did find her own "long distance friend," a young woman with lupus in Virginia.

To do

Comprehension & reflection

Roxanne Black has turned major personal setbacks into opportunities to help others. What characteristics does it take to respond that way to a personal crisis?

Have you ever had a personal setback that you turned into a way to help others? If you did, use your journal to write about what you did. If you didn't, write about what you *might* have done.

If you were ever very ill, would you want someone like yourself to talk to? Why or why not?

What do you think of organ donations? If you were old enough, would you sign an organ donor card? Why or why not?

Vocabulary

"Semi-annual" is a word that's been created by adding letters to the beginning of another word. These letters, called a "prefix," change the meaning of the word. What does the prefix "semi" mean? What other words can you think of that use this prefix? (Hint: using the dictionary *isn't* cheating!)

Think of a group of people who could be called a "network." What makes them a network?

Project possibilities

Log-on to *www.friendshealthconnection.org* and explore the website. What do you think of the services the network offers, and the responses from network members?

A Hero in Three Centuries

Hazel Wolf was born in Canada in 1898. When she was 14, she started sticking her neck out to make the world a better place, and she never stopped. She was commended as a Giraffe when she was 86 and kept right on sticking her neck out till her death at almost 102!

Back in 1912, Hazel thought it wasn't fair for her school to have sports for boys but not for girls. That's the way it was at almost all schools then, but Hazel didn't care if other people thought that was fine. She was sure it was wrong. She asked her school principal to let girls play basketball. He said he'd give her equipment and time on the school court if she could find ten girls who wanted to play—and he was sure she couldn't. But Hazel had ten girls waiting in the hall outside the principal's office! He was surprised, but he laughed and kept his promise.

All through her long life, Hazel surprised people, made them laugh, and got them to see things her way. She wanted people to be treated fairly, to have jobs, safe housing, peace, and a healthy environment. Over and over again, she got involved in issues that other people fight about and over and over again, Wolf found ways to get them to stop fighting, to laugh, and to cooperate.

She worked to save the last of the ancient trees in the Pacific Northwest. At the same time, she insisted that timber workers had to be trained for other jobs to do instead of felling and milling these trees, even though timber workers and environmentalists rarely help each other.

A nature lover, Wolf was a hiker and a kayaker. She also was an officer of the Seattle Audubon Society, a group that studies birds and protects the places where they live. Wolf started more new Audubon groups than anyone else in the entire US.

When she found that Native Americans and the big environmental groups weren't working together, she went to the tribal leaders and got them to join forces with groups like Audubon. Together they have a better chance of protecting the land, air and water that they all care so deeply about. In her late 90s, she began helping inner-city kids get involved in environmental protection efforts.

Wolf gave up decades of her private time for her causes, and all chances of making a prosperous living. She stood up to powerful people who didn't agree with her views on respecting working people and protecting the natural world. Through it all, she maintained her sense of humor, even when faced with going to jail for taking part in a peaceful protest. "I always thought if I ever went to jail, I'd get to work a jigsaw puzzle," she told the Giraffe Heroes Project. "But the one opportunity I had, I didn't get to finish it because someone bailed me out."

Many years ago, she almost lost her chance to be a US citizen because an immigration official called her a troublemaker. But to thousands of people, Hazel Wolf wasn't a troublemaker—she was a hero, speaking truth to power and spurring the powerless to action, decade after decade.

To do

Comprehension & reflection

Wolf used humor in her efforts to change the world. It's a tool that's available to all of us, and one that can be highly effective in improving a negative or tense situation. Have you ever gotten people to laugh instead of being angry? If you have, what happened? Describe some circumstances in which humor would *not* be appropriate.

Why would it be important that timber workers have other jobs to do? What does this suggest to you about Wolf's style of problem-solving? Consider a current problem in your school and think of a win-win solution for it, Hazel Wolf style.

Go to *http://members.tripod.com/~HazelWolf* to learn more about Wolf.

Vocabulary

Words that mean the same thing are called synonyms. What word in this story is a synonym for "collaborate"?

Words that have opposite meanings are called antonyms. What's an antonym for "respecting"? (Hint: You can make the word by using a prefix, letters added at the beginning of a word.)

Project possibilities

Wolf's concerns included equal treatment for girls and women, good jobs for everyone, a clean environment, and preserving habitat for birds. You could look into any of those that interest you and see what's already being done in each field. Is there a way you can assist an ongoing effort, or something you can do that isn't already being done?

Touchdown for Tolerance

In the small Idaho town of Marsing, football was everything. On Friday nights, hundreds of people from the town and the farms arou nd it would come to watch the Marsing Huskies play. **Ernesto "Neto" Villareal** was a star player on the high school team, good enough to be considered for a college athletic scholarship.

But the *fans* in Marsing were a problem. When any player did something good, everyone cheered, but if a Latino player made a mistake, people heckled them with ethnic insults like, "Stupid Mexican!" It happened a lot, and most people seemed not to notice.

But the Latino players noticed. They talked among themselves about being disrespected and treated differently than their Anglo teammates. Villareal convinced them that they shouldn't play anymore unless the insults stopped.

When they told their coach, he said they would only make things worse by refusing to play—the team couldn't win the state championship if the Latino players stopped playing. That would make *all* the fans angry with them. Villareal also knew that if the team stopped playing he could lose his chance at a football scholarship.

But stopping the insults meant more to Villareal than a scholarship. He talked to the student body president, who took the players' concerns to the principal. When the principal refused to do anything, the other Latino players thought there was nothing more they could do. They were ready to give up and resume playing. Not Villareal. He went over the principal's head to the School Board, even though he'd seen one of the School Board members *himself* shouting insults at Latino players. It was difficult to speak before this group of adults, but Villareal told them about the effects of the insults on the Latino players, and why they wouldn't play until something was done. "Now," he said, "they can't say nobody told them."

The student body president, inspired by Villareal's courage, wrote a letter on behalf of all the students, asking school officials to throw people out of the stadium if they yelled insults. Led by Villareal, the Latino players agreed that if the letter was read over the loudspeaker before the next game, they would play.

That next game was the big one—the homecoming game, with a parade, music and floats. The principal *refused* to read the letter, but the school superintendent overruled him and directed that the letter be read. When it was, people in the stadium stood and cheered. The full team came on the field for the kickoff. And the insults stopped.

Neto Villareal had scored a touchdown for tolerance. Combating racism in his town may have been the biggest win of his young life.

To do

Comprehension & reflection

Physical courage is about taking risks that might cause bodily injury. For many people, it's more frightening to be brave in a social situation, speaking up when others don't want you to do that, taking the chance of being disliked or of losing something you want very much. Imagine that you're Neto Villareal. What does it feel like to keep your teammates going when they want to give up, to speak to a School Board that includes one of the hecklers, to know that people are going to hate you if the team loses the championship? How hard do you think it was to risk his own chances for a scholarship?

Courage can be contagious. Who in this story was inspired by Villareal to be braver? Has anyone ever inspired you to be braver?

Vocabulary

The word "prejudice" combines the prefix "pre" with a root word from Latin. No nation speaks Latin today, but it is the source of many words in several modern languages. "Pre" means "before" and the Latin word "judice" means to judge. What does it mean to judge before?

Add the prefix "en" to the word "courage" and you've got the familiar word "encourage." What does the combination tell you about the meaning of the word?

Project possibilities

What might you do to encourage people to do something brave that helps others?

Is there a service project you might do that requires taking social risks such as speaking up to people who don't agree with you?

No More Dropouts

Calvin Bryant grew up on a Georgia farm, one of 16 kids of a sharecropper. He had to leave school in the 8th grade and go to work, because his family could not support him through more years in school. But Bryant never stopped learning.

Eventually he built up a prosperous furniture repair business in Sarasota, Florida. He's a success, providing economic advantages for his family and good jobs for his employees. His community named him Small Businessman of the Year.

That same year a teenager stole a lawnmower from Bryant's house. The thief was caught, and when Bryant went to court to identify him he told the judge, "Give him to me. I'll work with him." The judge thought he was nuts, but remanded the young man to Bryant's custody.

Bryant never doubted that the teen could turn his life around, and that belief rubbed off on the boy. Soon he was a valuable—and honest—employee in Bryant's company.

Pleased by this turnaround, Bryant began going into prisons as a counselor and bringing prisoners out, giving them good jobs, mentoring them, teaching them by his example that even a tough start in life doesn't have to stop a person who's determined to make it.

"They were making bad choices because they didn't know how to work with the system," Bryant says. "They didn't know what it had to offer, how to get what they needed *legally*."

A basic factor in that lack of knowledge was that most of them couldn't read and write. Bryant realized he could just work with lawbreakers forever, or he could also go straight for the next generation of potential prisoners—kids who were living in poverty and who weren't learning to read.

Bryant hired a teacher to run an after-school tutoring program for some of Sarasota's poorest kids. "I found out all kids at a very early age are very, very positive. They don't know about the 'can't-dos.'"

Bryant gives them positive reinforcement, good role models and a glimpse of life outside their own neighborhoods. He also gives them something to eat—he never knows if they get enough at home.

"These kids," Bryant says firmly, "will not be dropouts." And as good readers, their odds of being successful in life, like Calvin Bryant, go way, way up.

To do

Comprehension & reflection

Use the Internet or the library to find out about sharecroppers' lives. Would you use the word "prosperous" to describe these tenant farmers? Now see what you can find out about the lives of serfs in the Middle Ages. What similarities and differences do you see?

Do you agree with Bryant's view that "all kids at a very early age are very, very positive?" If you think he's right, how might that change the way children should be raised and educated?

Calvin Bryant overcame great difficulties to become a success in business. Instead of just enjoying the comforts he earned, he looked around to help others follow his lead out of poverty. Consider what the world would be like if everyone behaved this way. What changes can you imagine?

Studying or working with someone who believes in you and guides your efforts can make a huge difference in your chances of succeeding. Think of people in your life who have done this for *you*. Write to them about the effect they've had on your life. (Don't rule out members of your own family.)

Vocabulary

Did you look up "remanded" and add it to your vocabulary notes? If you didn't, are you *sure* you know what it means? Many words in general usage come from the professional jargon of lawyers, police officers and athletes. (Look up "jargon." It's a very useful word.) How is it that these words enter the general public's vocabulary?

Find the words in this story that are compound words— single words that are made of two words combined. (Hint: there are a lot of them.)

Project possibilities

Consider being a mentor to someone younger than you are. You could be an unofficial big brother or sister by just befriending kids who really need to know someone cares about them.

If you did mentor a younger student, you could write about your experiences and what they meant to you. This wouldn't be a huge project, but it could make a real difference in your life and in the life of one other person.

Patch Adams & friend.

A Pie in the Face of Greed

Patch Adams doesn't look like a doctor—he looks like a clown. He wears clown clothes, and has a mustache that curls out from his face. When he rides his unicycle and juggles, it's hard to picture him taking care of patients. But Adams is a hard-working doctor who is so concerned about the runaway costs of health care that he refuses to accept money from his patients.

When poor people get sick, they often can't afford medical care so they don't go to a doctor, or they do go to a doctor and then worry so much about how to pay the bill that they can get even sicker. Adams believes that worry is bad for people and that everyone should be able to go to a doctor when they need to. That's why he ran a free medical clinic in Arlington, Virginia, for 12 years.

Has anybody ever said *Gesundheit* to you when you sneeze? The German word *Gesundheit* means "good health." Adams called his free clinic the "Gesundheit Institute" because of its meaning and because the name made people laugh—he believes laughter is good for people's well-being.

Adams and another Gesundheit physician moonlighted in hospital emergency rooms and donated their salaries to keep the free clinic operating. People were so amazed that these doctors were doing this that many volunteered to help them run the clinic. During the dozen years it existed, the Gesundheit Institute took care of 15,000 patients, all gratis.

Now Patch Adams is building a new dream. The Gesundheit Center is in the hills of West Virginia and will have a complete hospital, houses and gardens, craft and exercise rooms. And it will all be free.

To pay the costs of building the new Center, Adams puts on his clown outfits and does a "Medicine Show," teaching people how to maintain their health. He performs all over the country and around the world in medical schools, hospitals, and anywhere people gather to learn. Since a movie was made about him, more people invite him to come and speak, and they add money to the funds that will complete the new hospital.

What Adams is doing is not always popular with other doctors. Some are embarrassed because he's "undignified." A few want to make as much money as possible, so when Adams says money isn't important, they find him irritating.

"We're giving away the most costly thing in America," Patch Adams says. "We're a pie in the face of greed."

Comprehension & reflection
What do you think Adams means when he says free medical care is a "pie in the face of greed"? If you've ever seen old "slapstick" comedy films, you've seen a lot of people get pies in their faces. What do the receivers of the pies usually have in common? (Hint: they tend to be people who have power and aren't using it wisely.)

What other things can be so costly that some of us can't afford them?

How important is it to you for a physician to be dignified?

Vocabulary
There are many commonly used words in our language that are not English. Think of three, and add them to your vocabulary notebook. (Hint: Some foreign words are used so often, you may not realize they aren't English. Ask your language teacher for some help on this one.)

The word "cycle" often takes a prefix. (Remember—a prefix is letters added to the beginning of a word that change its meaning.) What happens to the meaning of "cycle" when you add the prefix uni-, bi-, tri- or motor-?

How does the meaning of the word "dignified" change when you add the prefix "un"?

Write a sentence using the words "gratis" and "greed."

Project possibilities
Check out *www.patchadams.org* for ideas on service from Dr. Adams—and for some smiles.

Are there programs in your community to assist people who can't afford to buy basic necessities? (Hint: you could find out what assistance is being offered by service clubs, government agencies and religious institutions.)

Is there something that's *not* being offered that would be really important for people to have?

Doris Haddock, a.k.a. Granny D, third from the right, with people who joined her along her cross-country walk for clean government.

Walking Her Talk—A Long Long Way

There's nothing unusual about taking a walk. But if you're 89 years old and you have arthritis, emphysema, wear a steel back brace, and your "walk" is a 3,200-mile cross-country political statement, then it's amazing.

Doris Haddock (better known as "Granny D") is a former executive secretary who is not taking retirement sitting down. She's concerned over the role of campaign contributions in determining the outcome of political elections, and therefore the direction of our democracy. Haddock decided that she needed to do something dramatic to help rescue our democracy "from this sewer of cash and greed we've slipped into."

That something dramatic was her decision to "walk the talk" and travel, on foot, across the US talking to people about influence peddlers who've "set up their cash registers in our temple of democracy." Family members tried to talk her out of it, but she went right ahead, setting out from California and heading for Washington DC.

She logged 10 miles a day, through sandstorms, blizzards, blistering heat and torrential rains. She was hospitalized for dehydration after crossing the Mojave desert and risked hypothermia by skiing through snow in Maryland. Her emphysema made her lungs "sound like a teakettle" when she marched up a hill, but she kept walking.

And everywhere she walked, she talked. She told people all across the country that the candidate with the most money almost always wins. Often the winning candidate has over *ten times* as much money as the loser. Haddock told people that the voice of the common citizen was drowned out by companies and associations that showered cash on political candidates and then expected the winner to vote as these contributors want them to. She told her audiences that over $100 million dollars *a month* floods into Washington DC to influence politicians, adding, "You know where that leaves you and me, don't you?"

Haddock preached in churches, gave speeches, joined in parades, and appeared in newspapers and on radio and television. One of her admirers said that she motivated "tens of thousands of young people to get involved in civic life, and has inspired older people to stay involved in their communities."

Fourteen months later and just past her 90th birthday, "Granny D" arrived in Washington DC. Others might have taken a long rest after such a journey, but within days Haddock was arrested in the US Capitol building! Her "crime" was reading the Declaration of Independence, telling people we need now to declare "our independence from the corrupting bonds of big money in our election campaigns."

The judge could have given "Granny D" six months in prison and a $500 fine. Instead, he let her go, saying, "Take care, because it's people like you who will help America reach our destiny." She went right back to the Capitol building and read the Bill of Rights. Yes. She was arrested again.

On March 27, 2002, the landmark campaign finance reform Doris Haddock pushed for was signed into federal law. The following year, it was upheld by the Supreme Court. In the words of one US senator, "She's rebuilt our faith in the idea that one person can make a difference."

To do

Comprehension & reflection

A stereotype is a one-size-fits-all image of a group of people. Describe the stereotype "little old lady"? Does small, old Doris Haddock fit into that stereotype? What other stereotypes are common? How about older people's image of teen-agers? Do *you* fit into that stereotype?

How can campaign contributions affect the independence of our local, state and federal governments?

Consider the concept of civil disobedience. Its most famous role models are Martin Luther King, Jr. and Mohandas Gandhi. Using the Internet or the library, find out more about their lives, particularly the actions they took to change laws they believed to be unjust. Note that they, like Doris Haddock, deliberately but *non-violently* broke existing law, accepting the consequence of being arrested.

If the concept interests you, look up the history of the Suffragists in this country and in England. Hundreds of women were arrested for civil disobedience, before the laws were finally changed to allow women to vote.

What other causes can you find that have involved civil disobedience?

How do the words in the Declaration of Independence relate to civil disobedience?

Vocabulary

To figure out the meaning of the term "influence peddlers," look up each word separately. Now, what do you think the term means?

What is meant by the expression "walking your talk"?

The words "outcome," "sandstorm" and "landmark" are compound words. What other compound words can you make from "storm"? (Hint: Most of them are about weather, but not all.) Does "landmark," as it's used in this story, have anything to do with land?

Project possibilities

See what "Granny D" is up to at *www.grannyd.com*.

Toni Cordell-Seipel, whose story is on page 73, rollerskated across the country to bring attention to adult illiteracy. Many people walk or run to raise money for causes such as cancer research and child abuse prevention.

Is there any cause for which you'd be willing to go 3,200 miles? 320? 32? 3.2?

Dancing Into New Lives

Dora Andrade teaches poor kids in Fortaleza, Brazil, to dance—with their bodies, and with their hearts and minds.

In many societies, including Brazil's, formal ballet training is only for the children of the middle class and the wealthy. Some Brazilians were appalled by the idea of impoverished kids performing ballet in theatres, even telling Andrade that her "poor little creatures" would get nice theaters dirty or break things there. The doubters certainly weren't interested in attending a performance.

Now, Andrade's dancers are so renowned they play to sold-out audiences and are favorites of the nation's press. Their prominence helps them bring national attention to the plight of the poor, and their work with Dora Andrade brings the kids not only dance training but also meals, medical exams, dental care, vaccinations, computer training, etiquette lessons, confidence in their own abilities and hope for bettering their lives.

It's far more than Andrade envisioned doing when she opened her ballet school. But the girls arriving for class were so unhealthy, undernourished and listless, Andrade realized there was a lot they needed before they could dance.

Andrade had a reputation for pioneering—she'd staged ballets danced by pregnant women and by grandmothers, sometimes performing in public plazas. Faced now with rooms full of hungry girls, many of them ill, Andrade made the leap to be more than a ballet teacher to them.

Today, Andrade and her expanding staff teach more than 350 students each year—including boys—about music and theater and encourage them to read, maintain good grades and aspire to higher education. Andrade has enrolled more than 70 percent of the kids' *parents* in educational programs too. The Forteleza kids have performed before thousands of people and the school is being duplicated in other Brazilian cities.

The ultimate accolade? Andrade's school has grown so popular that some wealthy parents have tried to fake poverty in order to get their children enrolled.

 **To do**

Comprehension & reflection

Giraffe Dora Andrade is described as a pioneer in dance. Describe how she also became a pioneer in assisting needy kids.

Describe the actions of someone you think of as a pioneer. How did people respond to that pioneer?

Andrade realized that her students' basic needs should be met before they learned ballet. Do you think she was right? How does this idea apply to other forms of learning?

What basic needs do you think have to be met before kids are ready to learn new things? Can schools meet these needs? If not, who can?

Vocabulary

How do the words "envisioned" and "aspire" relate to being a dream builder?

If you had to *dance* a definition without speaking, how would you express "appalled"?

Project possibilities

If helping kids interests you, what might *you* do to help students be ready to learn?

Is there a service you could pioneer in your community?

They Speak for the Animals

A "sanctuary" is a place of safety, security and shelter, a place where one can live free from fear and pain. For many abused and neglected animals, sanctuary is a place called Pasado's Safe Haven, operated by Giraffe Heroes **Susan Michaels and Mark Steinway**.

Pasado's is their ranch in the mountains near Seattle, a rescue and rehabilitation site for pets and farm animals whose sad lives have been scarred, both mentally and physically, by cruelty or carelessness.

Any time of the day or night, Pasado's staff is ready to hit the road in their "AmMOOlance" truck to rescue animals that are in danger. The animals they pick up receive medical treatment if needed, plus food, water and loving care, all on Pasado's 50 acres of pastures and woodlands. There's no rush to recovery. Pasado's "guests" are welcome to spend the rest of their lives on the ranch, and no animal is ever put to sleep.

Michaels and Steinway both left well-paid urban careers to start Pasado's, using much of their own money to purchase the land and construct the buildings. They were prompted by the 1992 beating death of a gentle donkey named Pasado at a nearby farm.

The pair has since taken in hundreds of animals including mistreated horses, abandoned chickens, a couple of turkeys and a potbellied pig. They've also taken on animal abusers in court, testifying on their ill-treatment or neglect of animals. In the state legislature and in the US Congress, they fight for stiffer anti-cruelty laws and improved conditions at the factory farms that produce poultry and pork for the nation's markets.

Their outspokenness on behalf of animals has resulted in threats to themselves and their property from people who resent their insistence that all animals be treated with dignity, even those that are going to be killed for the nation's markets.

Michaels and Steinway offer educational programs on animal care and on how to create sanctuaries such as Pasado's Safe Haven throughout the world.

It all means long hours, angry reactions from abusers, and a constant struggle to pay the bills, but Susan Michaels and Mark Steinway look at the animals they're caring for and know they're doing just what they want to do. "The rewards far outweigh the pain," says Michaels.

To do

Comprehension & reflection

Use the Internet or the library to learn the history of sanctuaries. If you were in danger, where would you go for sanctuary? Have you ever provided sanctuary to a person or an animal? If you have, what happened?

Susan Michaels and Mark Steinway are so concerned about protecting animals, they've raised their voices to testify for changes in their state's laws. Is there something you're that concerned about? If there is, what is it and what changes would you speak out for?

Vocabulary

How does the prefix "anti-" change the word "cruelty"? Invent two other words using this prefix. (Hint: think of things you're against, even if they're not serious. Examples might be "anti-broccoli" or "anti-homework.")

What's the difference between the terms "taking in" and "taking on"?

The words "haven" and "heaven" are close both in spelling and in meaning. See if you can find a historical link between them. (Hint: your favorite librarian can help you find the history of how words have evolved over the centuries.)

Project possibilities

If taking care of animals interests you, go to *www.pasadosafehaven.org* and consider the advice there on how to start a safe haven in your neighborhood.

Are there *people* in your community who need shelter? What services exist for them? Are there ways you can assist shelters for the homeless or places that serve food to people who are hungry?

If there are no such services, your class could find out about the needs that aren't being met and speak out for public or private programs that will fill the gaps.

The Earth Angels, with their director, Neal Andre.

Photo by Paul Childress

Saving the Earth,
One Vacant Lot at a Time

"My neighborhood is bad. I see people dump trash on the ground so they don't have to walk to the dumpsters. There are a lot of gangs and lots of shooting. People sell drugs on the corner and this scares me. If I see something I shouldn't, then they might kill me to keep me from telling the police. I might also get shot by accident."

That's an eleven-year-old girl describing her neighborhood in East St. Louis, Missouri. Life is so difficult and dangerous there, most people think there's nothing that can be done.

But not the **Earth Angels**. That's a club for kids who are growing up in this tough place. The club started in 1987 and hundreds of kids have joined since then, to defend the earth—and their own neighborhood.

Some people said the club would never work. These kids had so much trouble to deal with right in East St. Louis, how could they do anything for the earth? But the kids have proved those people wrong.

In the neighborhood, they do recycling work that cleans up the streets and the vacant lots *and* earns money they use to make the neighborhood look better. In just two years, the Angels collected and recycled 49,000 pounds of glass, over 200,000 aluminum cans, more than 700 old tires, hundreds of batteries, and 93 shopping carts! They found all this stuff on the streets, in empty lots, and in dumpsters.

They used the recycling money to buy seeds, plants and gardening tools. Thanks to the Angels, empty lots all over the neighborhood are becoming little parks. The Angels thought people would like these places, and they do. The amazing thing is that wildlife is attracted to them too. "We have birdfeeders and birdbaths in our wildlife habitats, where we can watch cardinals, chickadees, blue jays—lots of different birds," said Earth Angel Lela Ford. The mini-parks have also attracted raccoons, opossums and a family of red foxes!

Each Angel works four or five hours a week during the school year and much more during the summer. Other kids laugh at them and tease them when they see them working on their projects. The Angels have learned to ignore this and keep going. Sometimes they do the same work over and over. They clean up a place just to find it trashed a few days later. But the Angels don't quit. They say that if they don't keep coming back, the neighborhood will never get better.

To earn money for their projects, the kids have rummage sales, sell buttons and T-shirts, and invite people to buy memberships in Earth Angels. People all over the country have joined! The kids send money to groups that protect dolphins, whales and rainforests all over the world.

One Earth Angel project is especially beautiful and, at the same time, very sad. The kids plant a tree for each St. Louis child who has died violently. There are already over 60 tree in the "Forest of Life."

Thanks to Earth Angels, people in the neighborhood have beautiful little parks. They know that the children care about their community. The Forest of Life tells them that too many children are dying—and that the violence must stop.

To do

Comprehension & reflection
The Earth Angels send money out of their community to help environmental groups, even though their own neighborhood has so many needs. Why do you think they do that? If you were an Earth Angel, would you be for or against this? Why?

How do you think the Forest of Life affects people who see it?

This story starts out with a description of this neighborhood by an eleven-year-old girl. Imagine you're just 11; describe *your* neighborhood. What needs improvement?

Vocabulary

Even when you already know a word, you can learn more about it in a dictionary or online. Look up a familiar word from this story and see if you learn something new about it. Now keyboard the unusual word "cetaceans" into a search engine and see which of the familiar words in the story come up. Surprised?

Find the compound words (two words put together to make one, remember?) in this story.

You may have heard the expression, "A picture is worth a thousand words." Make pictures in your journal of the wildlife you observe in your neighborhood. (You could also use some words to label the creatures you draw.)

Project possibilities

If you and your classmates started cleaning up an area and planting flowers, how do you think other people would react?

Go to *www.hometown.aol.com/tambo* for activity ideas from the Earth Angels.

One of the biggest challenges to doing good things in a community is having to raise money. How do the Earth Angels raise money? Keep their methods in mind if you have to raise money to do a project in *your* community.

The Grace to Go On

Why would a new doctor and his wife leave a beautiful home in a beautiful city to live in the poorest and most desolate place in America?

Andy Hurst needed to work in a rural area for just one month, as part of his medical training. Many medical schools require rural service because there's such a shortage of doctors outside of the nation's cities.

Andy and Vashti Hurst chose South Dakota's Pine Ridge Indian reservation, which is almost the size of Connecticut and is home to over 40,000 Oglala Lakota Sioux Indians. There, the Hursts saw things they found hard to believe: elderly, disabled women trying to survive in tents during blizzards; tiny, run-down shacks housing 25 people; children whose only drinking water was in the backs of toilets. On Pine Ridge, thousands are without housing, 60% live below the poverty level, and there's a 65% dropout rate in the schools. Approximately a third of the houses have no electricity or running water and the unemployment rate is close to 90%. All this affects people's health severely. And although the need is great, there are just a few physicians in the reservation's 4,000 square miles.

After returning to their comfortable Seattle home, the Hursts couldn't stop thinking about what they'd seen. The idea of building a prosperous practice in the city was no longer attractive to them. They returned to Pine Ridge, not for a short stay, but to live and work. "Doc Andy" as he is now called, became one of those few physicians willing to stay and serve the people of the reservation.

Doc Andy practices medicine and, together, the Hursts work at the National Association for American Indian Children and Elders (NAAICE) a nonprofit they founded that runs 30 support programs. They coordinate the efforts of volunteers who travel from all over the world to assist in NAAICE's work.

That work includes delivering supplies to mothers with new babies, and providing people with firewood, propane, food and clothing. It involves helping families install water and sewer systems and build outhouses. It's also distributing books to schools, organizing youth activities, sponsoring athletic events, and even assisting with funeral expenses.

NAAICE policies include a strong belief in self-help. A home ownership program requires residents to pay for rebuilt trailers purchased for them by NAAICE so that more trailers can be rebuilt for others. It's difficult, but Vashti Hurst says that once the debt has been paid, families have "met a responsibility to themselves and to their community. That's empowerment."

Off the reservation, the Hursts have become messengers to the entire world, informing non-Indians of what they call the "ongoing reservation crisis throughout the United States of America." The Hursts receive no salary from NAAICE for their 100-hour work weeks. Instead, they pay for much of the organization's work out of their own pockets.

When observers ask how they can continue in the face of such overwhelming poverty, Andy and Vashti Hurst have a powerful answer. They go on because the Oglala Lakota Sioux go on. "They are people of great dignity and grace."

To do

Comprehension & reflection

What do you know about the history of indigenous people in the Americas? In the library or on the Internet, look up the history of the Oglala Lakota Sioux. How did they come to be living on this land that has no resources to sustain them?

Sitting Bull and Crazy Horse will appear in the stories you find. What were the lives of the Oglala Lakota Sioux like when these leaders were alive?

Consider the lives of the people of Pine Ridge from the viewpoint of these long dead leaders.

Vocabulary

An acronym is a word formed from the initials of a name. Many organizations give themselves names that make easy-to-say acronyms. People call NAAICE "nais" rather than saying each of the letters. As you go through this book, you'll find many groups that have such acronyms. Watch for LOVE, SHIP, ACORN, SWaMP and SAVE.

Project possibilities

Check out *www.pineridgerez.net/naaice.php* for more information on the work going on at Pine Ridge.

If there are any reservations in or near your community, find out what the conditions are for the people living there. Some reservations are actually prospering; most are not. If a reservation near you is poor, are there any organizations like NAAICE assisting people? If there are, do they have programs you'd like to take part in? If there aren't, would you be interested in *starting* an assistance program?

Dolly Kiffin, center, guides visiting officials through Broadwater Farms.

Taking Charge of Home Ground

When **Dolly Kiffin** stuck her neck out to change her world, she described herself as "just a housewife," a Jamaica-born dressmaker raising six children at Broadwater Farm, a huge housing project near London. The project was dirty, decaying and dangerous. The young, who were mostly without jobs, terrorized the old, who hid in their apartments. Tensions between black and white tenants, already high, intensified after the head of the tenants' association appeared on television spouting white-supremacist prejudices.

Kiffin wanted to end the hatred she saw in Broadwater Farm. She thought a sense of community could grow among the 3,000 residents of the project if they tackled their problems together, and they could start by helping the unemployed young people.

The Broadwater Farm Youth Association (BFYA) was formed after Kiffin led a series of meetings in her apartment. The first priority of the BFYA was creating a youth center. With a small grant from a local government agency, the Broadwater kids renovated an old fish and chips shop under the guidance of a local contractor, learning valuable building skills in the process.

From the beginning, Kiffin insisted that the BFYA center had to be something that would help bring the whole community together. When the kids wanted money for a pool table and arcade games, for example, Kiffin made a deal with them. They could have the equipment, but half the profits from the games had to be used to provide meals for senior citizens in the project. The BFYA not only took on the meals program but also provided drivers for day trips the kids organized for the elderly. Young and old, blacks and whites, began to know one another.

Kiffin wasn't done yet. She said that government programs had been training young people for jobs that didn't exist. She suggested that the BFYA create jobs by training people to work for themselves. The young people in

BFYA started small cooperative businesses that they owned and ran. As these businesses grew, they hired and trained new people. Over 100 young people were soon employed in seven co-op businesses that provided vital community services, and more co-ops were starting. Kiffin got a community garden going and pressured the local government into requiring that people from Broadwater Farm be hired to maintain it.

To the embarrassment of social-welfare experts and government bureaucrats, Dolly Kiffin's work has been extremely successful. She proved that low-income people could help themselves with only a minimum of government support. "We hadn't any qualifications at all," she said, "just our love for people. We put our whole selves into it."

Kiffin worked for years without pay. She now receives a salary, which she returns to the BFYA general fund. "I do it out of love for people," she says in her strong Jamaican accent, "regardless of what race they are—black or white or whatever. I did it out of determination, for I could not sit down and accept racism. I do it to show that ordinary grassroots people can do something to stop racism."

To do

Comprehension & reflection

In this story, the people of Broadwater figured out their problems and got to work on solving them. What are the advantages of people in a difficult situation finding their own solutions rather than having an outsider tell them what to do?

On the Internet or in the library, look into the history of supremacism. Where and when has it appeared, and what have the results been? (Hint: You'll find far too many examples to take them all in. Focus on a few and see what they have in common.) Is there supremacist thinking in your community, now?

When you meet someone old or someone whose race is different from your own, do you assume you know who they are and what they think? Do they seem to feel they know who *you* are and what *you* think? Are they right? Are you?

What are the similarities and differences between the prejudice shown in this story and that in Neto Villareal's story on page 5?

Vocabulary

Alliteration is the writing technique of repeating initial consonants. The writer of this story describes the housing project as "dirty, decaying and dangerous." Choose three alliterative words to describe the place where *you* live.

How would you describe a supremacist? What almost complete word do you see within "supremacist" that gives you a clue to its meaning?

Project possibilities

Are there needs in your community that could be met by people of differing ages or races working together?

What problems does your school class have that you might solve on your own rather than waiting for someone else to give you a solution?

A Friend Afar

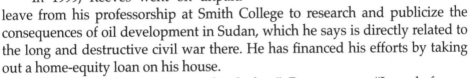

Eric Reeves has put his job, his income, and his reputation on the line to fight for the people of Sudan, people he's never met, in a country he's never visited.

In 1999, Reeves went on unpaid leave from his professorship at Smith College to research and publicize the consequences of oil development in Sudan, which he says is directly related to the long and destructive civil war there. He has financed his efforts by taking out a home-equity loan on his house.

"I desperately want peace for Sudan," Reeves says. "I work for no organization; I haven't taken money from anyone.... I have no secret mandate or agenda."

Reeves' teaching life in Northampton, Massachusetts, was about as far removed from Sudan as possible. He taught Shakespeare and Renaissance English, and, in his spare time, he contributed wood-turnings he made to charitable organizations such as Doctors Without Borders, a group that delivers emergency aid to victims of armed conflict, epidemics and natural and man-made disasters. It was through that group that he first heard about the Sudan conflict.

"I know when I've seen a morally unambiguous situation and this is it," Reeves said, explaining that two million people have died, five million are refugees and the remaining Sudanese endure famine, disease, enslavement and military aggression. Reeves' research has prompted him to publish dozens of essays in international publications and to give interviews to international media, such as the BBC, CBC, and *The New York Times*. He has testified before the US House International Relations Committee, the Congressional Human Rights Caucus, and the Commission on International Religious Freedom. His efforts have been met with public criticism of him from the State Department, Wall Street, and the Sudan's government in Khartoum.

Reeves believes his battle for human rights over oil-company profits is bringing the invisible war in Sudan to the forefront of US foreign policy.

"We'll see what one very loud, very committed, very passionate voice can accomplish," says Eric Reeves, "if it's really, really focused, and it just doesn't give up."

To do

Comprehension & reflection

What are the advantages and disadvantages of this Giraffe Hero's never having seen the Sudan?

What other heroes in this book have stuck their necks out for people they don't know?

As in Doris Haddock's story on page 13, the term "special interests" is used to describe groups who try to influence governmental policies because they have an interest in the outcome. They're often corporations with business interests, or associations with their members' interests at stake. Is Reeves' work a "special interest"? Why or why not?

Vocabulary
What does it mean to put something "on the line"?

Inside the word "publicize" there's the word "public." What does that tell you about what it means to publicize something?

Give an unambiguous fact about your school. Does everyone in your class agree that what you say is accurate? If they don't, is the fact you chose really unambiguous?

Give an example of an international issue. Now name a national issue. What does the prefix "inter" mean?

Project possibilities
Is there a problem somewhere in the world that you're concerned about? If there is, you could look into ways you might help solve that problem.

A Latina for the 'Glades

Darlene Rodriguez likes to challenge stereotypes. Like the ones that say teens can't be community leaders, or that girls shouldn't be taken seriously. Or the belief that minority groups don't care about the environment.

Rodriguez also likes tackling big issues. As a high school student, she became concerned about the Everglades, near her home in Florida. The Everglades are a vast and slow-moving river, a thin layer of fresh water in south Florida that once was larger than seven Rhode Islands. It's now 60 miles wide, 200 miles long, and six inches deep. In that reduced area, an amazing array of rare animals and plants still survive, including many found nowhere else on earth.

Years ago most people thought of the Everglades as a useless swamp. They drained off the water and used the land for other things. Farms, housing developments and golf courses have eaten into the Everglades for decades, destroying irreplaceable habitat for wildlife, and the natural movement of water.

When she began researching "the glades," one of the things Rodriguez learned was that without them, south Florida would be a desert—evaporation from the Everglades provides 80% of the rainfall for south Florida.

The more Rodriguez learned, the more she wanted to protect the Everglades. She worked for the Friends of the Everglades environmental group and ran her school's Science Honors Society, bringing the preservation of the glades to the Society's agenda. Although friends would have preferred her company at the movies or the mall, she spent her free time on her cause.

When a severe drought hit south Florida, she knew that there would be even less water to keep the Everglades alive and that it would be essential for everyone to conserve water.

The Spanish-speaking population of south Florida is very large—in the county where Rodriguez lives 60% of the students are Latino. Rodriguez observed that many of them didn't know much about the environment, but she wouldn't accept the stereotype that they didn't *care*. She knew that they would want to help when they learned what was at stake. She decided to find environmental information in Spanish that she could give Spanish-speaking students and adults in the community but, "I discovered that there was very little Spanish language literature on the environment, preservation, and conservation." What little did exist was mostly outdated.

Rather than give up, Rodriguez wrote a brochure herself, in both Spanish and English, to inform Spanish-speaking citizens and inspire them to help solve environmental problems. She spent many hours researching the brochure, and persuaded the Friends of the Everglades to pay for its production. She also got the Science Honors Society to help her do neighborhood surveys to discover which environmental topics were of greatest community interest.

Rodriguez found that being a pioneer has a price. Because of her age, some adults criticized her, saying, "You're too young. You don't know anything." She was ridiculed by some non-Latinos because she has an accent when she speaks English. Some people told her to "go back where you came from." (Rodriguez was born in Latin America and spoke Spanish as her first language.)

But Rodriguez persisted. She learned from the surveys that many Latinos were interested in the environment, but needed more information and guidance on subjects like water conservation, endangered species, and protecting the Everglades. She wrote the brochure to include those issues and then added specific suggestions on how individuals and families could make a difference. She said, "Kids at school will use it to educate their parents, who'll then take it to their workplaces, friends, and churches."

Rodriguez also made presentations at her school emphasizing how easy it was to conserve water. She created an "ecommercial," an environmental public service announcement that played on her school's closed-circuit TV. It included a jingle she wrote called "Every Drop Counts." Water use at the school dropped, helping Rodriguez make her point that when Latinos understood the problem, they would do the right thing.

The time Rodriguez spent on conservation was a gamble with her personal future. Coming from a low-income family, her best chance of attending a good college was getting the highest possible grades so she could win a full scholarship. Still, she gave up study time to devote endless hours to her cause. She decided that the survival of the Everglades was more important than whether or not one girl went to a prestigious college.

Rodriguez recalls the book on the Everglades that she read when she was only 11, *A River of Grass*. The first sentence in that book is always in her mind: "There are no other Everglades in the world." This one remarkable girl's B average and her stunning record of community service got her into college, and her championing of the Everglades earned her the friendship of her personal hero, fellow Giraffe Marjory Stoneman Douglas, the author of *A River of Grass*.

To do

Comprehension & reflection

Darlene Rodriguez's actions were influenced by a book she read when she was very young. Is there a book or a film that has influenced your actions?

Who is your personal hero? What has that person done to make the world a better place?

As in many stories in this book, stereotyping is a big part of Darlene's story. What stereotypes did she have to break through? Are there stereotypes you've had to overcome so that people understand who you are and what you can do?

Vocabulary

"Ecommercial" probably won't be in your dictionary, because the word was invented to describe commercials like the ones Darlene did. What other environmental words begin with "eco"?

Project possibilities

What could you do to inspire kids younger than you are to do something positive for their world?

Create an "ecommercial" about an environmental issue that concerns you. Present it at a school assembly, a parent/teachers' meeting, and/or a public gathering in your community.

Find out what the water issues are in your community. If there's a river, lake, or groundwater supply that needs to be protected, are there any groups working on that? If there are, how could you assist them? If there aren't, does the issue interest you as the subject of a project you could create?

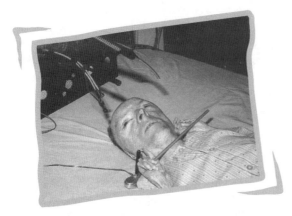

Forty-one Pounds of Courage

We've all heard that "beauty is only skin deep." We *know* that character and spirit are more important than how people look. Still, many of us turn our eyes away from people who have disabilities or disfigurements. We don't even stop to wonder who they are and what they think; we don't imagine that they might be some of the most interesting people we could ever know.

Giraffe **Daryl Smith** was just such a person. Smith was a man so physically disabled that most people in such condition spend their lives hidden away by relatives or in nursing homes, invisible to the rest of the world and taking no part in it. Smith was struck by a wasting muscular condition when he was seven years old. He had to leave school and spent many years in the privacy of his room. But his intelligence, his strong spirit, and his concern for other people with disabilities were too large to stay hidden away.

For years, only Smith's warm voice left his room—over the phone and on the ham radio he operated, making friends all over the world. If you had talked to him, you'd have heard a soft-spoken, good-humored, quick-witted Southern gentleman. Smith was all these things, but he was also blind, couldn't walk, and weighed 41 pounds.

"I had a very rich fantasy life," Smith told us when he got his Giraffe commendation. "In my fantasy world I was free to do anything I wished. I flew planes, sailed ships, commanded armies and played football for Auburn University."

Smith's life began to change when he signed up to take a college course offered on TV. An administrator at the college was so impressed by Smith's determination to learn, he audio-taped the written lessons for him, and talked friends into teaching Smith other courses.

Smith was able to speed up his schoolwork when the state of Alabama bought him an environmental control system that enabled him to operate telephones, tape decks and other machines. He used the equipment to tape classes, and earned an Associate degree entirely by telephone. He not only got the degree, he earned a *summa cum laude,* the highest academic honor.

Smith pushed and poked and prodded the Alabama Vocational Rehabilitation Service to support further schooling. He wanted to study psychology and to help other people with severe disabilities. He earned his Bachelor's degree, by phone, and set out to get a Master's degree. To get that credential, he had to leave home, to live among strangers and work with even more strangers every day. One of those strangers was a high-tech engineer.

The engineer was so impressed by Smith that he created an improved, portable, environmental control system that he named the DS-2000, after Daryl Smith. He and Smith and a computer programmer worked all the bugs out of the system together. The patent on the final system lists the engineer, the programmer, and Daryl Smith.

"My job is either guinea pig or test pilot. Test pilot sounds better," Smith told us with a laugh.

Smith's Giraffe commendation was for his many years of going out into the world to help others. He helped the University of Alabama improve its independent living facilities for the severely disabled, making the way easier for other eager learners who needed extra help. Most amazingly, he met with community groups to show them what he could do with the DS-2000, and encourage them to donate the system to others who needed it. How did he feel about meeting with strangers?

"It used to bother me, but it doesn't bother me any more," he told us. "If enough of us are seen in public, then people are gonna know we're there... I want to show folks what even the most severely physically disabled people can do... Here I am—all 41 pounds!"

A lot of people who met Daryl Smith will never forget him, and all he could and did do for others.

To do

Comprehension & reflection

Daryl Smith is portrayed here as a person who not only was smart, determined and caring, but also had a fine sense of humor. Does his story match your expectations about a person with such severe disabilities?

It's easy to see physical beauty, and difficult to know the beauty of a person's spirit or character. The next time you see someone who isn't attractive, what if you remembered Daryl Smith and gave yourself a chance to discover that unattractive person's strengths?

Vocabulary
The words "pushed and poked and prodded" are used in this story. Alliteration was also used in the Earth Angels story on page 20, remember? Look for other examples of alliteration in things that you read. (Hint: It's particularly common in advertising.) Choose an initial sound and a subject and make up your own series of alliterative words. For instance, "ch" and "adjectives about my little brother" could give you "choosy, childish and chubby."

You won't find "gonna" in the dictionary, but we all know what it means. What other words are sometimes written as they're said in everyday speech even though they're not officially words? (Hint: There's always "woulda, shoulda, coulda.")

How does the prefix "in" change the meaning of a word such as "visible"? What other words can you think of that have their meanings changed by adding "in"? (Just for fun, how about "flammable"? English is sometimes a strange language.)

Project possibilities
Smith was greatly helped in his education and in his efforts to assist others by people who cared about him. Find out if there are people with disabilities in your community who could use some assistance. If no one is providing it, what might you do?

Walking As Tall As Trees

Wangari Maathai, a professor of biology at Nairobi University in Kenya, could simply enjoy the prestige and security of being a highly educated, well-paid woman in a country where most women lead far different lives. Instead, she founded a movement that has set out to transform those women's lives and the entire economy of her nation. This is clearly a positive mission, but it has put Maathai in great personal danger.

Her Green Belt Movement has enlisted over 80,000 rural women in planting and tending over 20 million trees. Everywhere that the movement is strong, the villages and the countryside are green with gracious trees that give bananas, mangoes, and papayas to people who remember starvation and malnutrition. The people in these areas see that their own local women have brought about this transformation to health, beauty and economic independence. But to the one-party government of strongman Daniel Arap Moi, such independence is "subversive."

President Moi has blamed Maathai for giving so many people the idea that they can take charge of their own lives; he has had her imprisoned repeatedly for defying his dictatorship, but she will not be silenced.

Working in the city as well as the countryside, she organized demonstrations to stop the building of a skyscraper in Nairobi's only park. Moi put her in jail again, but the people's protest and her letters to the building's financiers caused them to withdraw from the project.

The city of Nairobi still has a people's park. And in the country, the women of the Green Belt tend their trees, feed their families, and walk tall—like Wangari Maathai.

This story was written when Professor Maathai was named a Giraffe Hero in 1990. As of this printing, her Green Belt Movement has established over 600 community networks throughout Kenya, each network planting trees and changing the country's economy. President Moi is out of the government and Professor Maathai is in, winning a seat in Kenya's Parliament with 98% of the vote. In 2004 she became the first environmentalist and the first African woman ever to win the Nobel Peace Prize.

To do

Comprehension & reflection

Look up dictatorships on the Internet or in the library. Describe the differences between dictatorships and democracies. Why do dictators dislike independent thinking and actions by the people they rule? What did you learn in your search about other dictators' punishment of people who do their own thinking?

Go to *www.greenbeltmovement.org* and see what Maathai and the women she leads are doing now. Many progressive economic movements in the world's poorer nations are being carried out by women. If this interests you, research the success of the Grameen Bank in Bangladesh, which helps women develop small businesses to support their families.

Vocabulary

Why can trees be seen as "gracious"?

How can independence be subversive?

Why do you think Professor Maathai's work is called the Green Belt Movement?

Project possibilities

Consider something you'd like to transform in your school. Why do you want it to be different than it is? Describe what it would be like if it were transformed.

Professor Maathai's transformation work is described as bringing health, beauty, and economic independence to Kenya. These are all results of environmental changes. What environmental change might benefit the health, beauty, and/or economic independence of *your* community? (Hint: it doesn't have to be a huge change to make a real difference.)

Leaving Out Violence

Twinkle Rudberg was walking down a Montreal street with her husband Daniel when they saw a teen-aged boy assault an elderly woman and snatch her purse. Mr. Rudberg chased the thief into a park, where the boy stabbed his pursuer in the heart.

As a widow raising young children and working to support them, Twinkle Rudberg spent years dealing with the emotional and practical aftermath of the killing, and pondering the dynamics that would lead a 14-year-old boy to murder. Then, her children grown, she took what she had learned and set out to end youth violence—*her* way.

"The more backlash you have against them, the more you'll have youth crime," Rudberg decided. "What these troubled kids need is a community and a voice."

Her nonprofit, LOVE (Leave Out ViolencE), welcomes kids who have had their own violent experiences, both as victims and as perpetrators. In Rudberg's programs, they all learn about anger-management, conflict-resolution, and leadership, using photojournalism and writing to produce a newspaper called One LOVE.

The paper is harsh and unblinking, as the kids depict experiences of mutilations, rapes and beatings. But through all the horror, a bright spirit shines—Twinkle Rudberg's conviction that at-risk kids can learn and change and live meaningful lives. The kids take in her belief in them and begin to believe in themselves. Kids who complete the program use their new skills and their new attitude to become teachers of other at-risk kids.

One person observing what she has done said, "It's especially inspiring when a person who's been deeply injured reacts as Ms. Rudberg has. There are far too many stories of revenge and bitterness—we need to see there's another way, one that stops the cycle of harm. Ms. Rudberg is ending the violence, so that others don't suffer."

There is now a LOVE book, and a traveling art show of works by the students in the program. LOVE has worked in schools in Toronto and Montreal and has been awarded government grants to fund LOVE programs in Ontario, Quebec, Halifax and Vancouver.

Comprehension & reflection

Losing someone you love to violence is a deeply emotional experience. Many people in Twinkle Rudberg's situation are overwhelmed by grief or by anger. Consider the thoughts and feelings she may have had as she turned her life toward helping teens deal with violence.

Rudberg wanted to understand the "dynamics" that would lead a 14-year-old boy to commit murder. All of us have factors in our lives that could be considered our lives' dynamics.

What dynamics do you think Rudberg was dealing with? If you were her, what would *you* have felt? What would you have *done*?

Think of someone you admire. What are the dynamics in that person's life?

Ask four people what they do to control themselves when they're angry. If any of them share an anger-management strategy, what is it? Did anyone have a unique strategy? What was it?

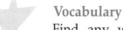

Vocabulary

Find any words in this story that are not completely familiar to you. See if you can understand their meanings by the way they're used in the story. Then look them up in a dictionary and put them in your vocabulary notebook, with a brief definition of each one. Use each word in a sentence that you make up yourself.

New words are constantly being added to our language, sometimes by combining familiar words to make a compound word. When the words are combined, they're hyphenated. As the new combination becomes more and more familiar, the hyphen often disappears. Find examples of both kinds of compound words in this story. Make up some compound words of your own.

Project possibilities

Go to *www.leaveoutviolence.com* to learn more about how Rudberg works with troubled kids. Are there any ideas there that you could use to help your community?

One of the compound words in this story is photojournalism, which means reporting a story in photographs. Is there a situation in your community that could be reported in photographs? Who's got a camera?

A Great Son of Two Nations

Franklin "Chaskae" (pronounced *CHESS-kay*) **McCabe III** is proud of his Navajo and Sioux ancestors and wants the best for all Native Americans. "Chaskae" means "first-born son," which is what he is in his family.

It upset him to see people using drugs and alcohol. He knew substance abuse was a serious problem in his hometown, Parker, Arizona, which is on a tribal reservation. Many public events there were sponsored by beer companies. Chaskae saw drugs and alcohol destroying families and taking away people's hope.

At 13, he started organizing drug-free high school dances in Parker. He was the disc jockey, borrowing his father's sound equipment and inviting teens to come dance to their favorite music. Parker kids did come, and Chaskae started putting on dances for kids in other reservation towns. He called his service "Chaskae D.J." and said his intention was "to do whatever it takes to make a small or large impact on my peers."

Chaskae had two big goals in life. He wanted to get really good grades so he could go to college, and he wanted to stop Native American kids from getting into substance abuse. He was smart and liked studying, so he was used to getting top grades in school. But he knew he couldn't do that and also work against substance abuse as much as he wanted to.

So he made a difficult decision—to be satisfied with some lower grades. He would divide his time between studying and his anti-abuse campaign. Taking such a risk with his own future wasn't easy. But showing teens that they can have fun without alcohol and drugs—and heading them away from ruining their lives—was worth it to him.

By the time he was 16, he was taking a complete sound and light show all over Arizona, Utah, Wyoming, Colorado, Idaho and Montana. He worked in abuse-prevention groups and he talked with kids about their personal problems with drugs and alcohol. He explained his concerns to parents and officials. He started a youth club at his school. He did so much good work that the governor of Arizona asked him to be a member of a state committee on preventing drug abuse by the young.

In spite of his decision to give so much time to his cause, Chaskae was accepted to Stanford, a university that requires very high grades. We think they were impressed with his intelligence and his devotion to helping his people. He studied there to be a filmmaker so he could make movies that tell the world how brave and smart and caring his people are. That's a pretty good description of one young Navajo-Sioux named Chaskae McCabe.

To do

Comprehension & reflection

On the Internet or in the library, find out about the effects of substance abuse on Native American communities, and the history of their nations since the arrival in the Americas of Europeans. What role might despair have in substance abuse?

How has Chaskae's hope for the future affected his actions and his community?

In what ways is this story different from that of the Hursts on page 23?

In your community, how much do adults' actions affect what young people do?

Vocabulary

Several words in this story have hyphens to mark the addition of prefixes or the compounding of words. How are the words' meanings affected by these hyphenations?

Project possibilities

If there are kids in your community abusing drugs or alcohol, is there anything you or your class might do to affect their attitudes and their actions?

What about Chaskae McCabe's idea of organizing events where no drugs or alcohol are involved? Would that work in your community? Why or why not?

Angela Martinez, center, with a SHIP construction crew.

The SHIP That Raised a Roof

When **Angela Martinez** (center, in the photo) of Tampa, Florida, was 54 and her four children were grown, she found herself newly divorced, a classic "displaced homemaker." As she dealt with all the changes in her life, she volunteered at a local women's center, where she assisted other women who were learning to redirect *their* lives.

One of Martinez' clients told her that she had no money to repair her roof after a tree fell on it. Martinez, who had done home repair jobs when she was a kid, talked two other women into helping her rebuild the roof. Although none of them had any professional construction experience, they did the job successfully, thrilling both themselves and their elderly client. Martinez saw a match between the need for jobs for displaced homemakers and the need for housing repairs for the elderly poor.

She launched the Senior Home Improvement Program, a free home-repair service for seniors "womanned" by a graying crew of four. Martinez told us, "Starting SHIP was really scary. I had never done anything like this before. I had just become a displaced homemaker…and I was in a very fragile state."

Martinez and her crew took a lot of razzing from the men in the local construction industry for being female, middle-aged and inexperienced. When they tackled their first job—a collapsed floor—the local building inspector said, "You know how to *wash* a floor, but what makes you think you can *replace* one?" They consulted books, asked questions and built a fine strong floor.

The SHIP women find that they are good role models for the older women whose homes they repair. The sight of the SHIP crew hauling plywood and roofing materials up ladders and across beams has inspired many a woman to abandon her feelings of helplessness and get moving again.

Martinez left the work crew to do the office work of managing the expanding program. She's found the grant money to pay the SHIP repair team as well as a weatherization crew, a heavy-chore crew and a plumber. She started an Adopt-a-Home Program that recruits businesses to help pay for materials.

Conquering yet another level of fear, this once-shy woman did a weekly home-repair segment on a local TV show. Women who were afraid their lives were over when their marriages ended saw what Angela Martinez did and realized that they too could make new lives.

To do

Comprehension & reflection

Angela Martinez described herself as in a fragile state when she started helping other women. Have there been times when you've felt fragile? How hard would it be to take on a new challenge when you feel that way? What might be the advantages of assisting others at such a time? The disadvantages?

Most of the people in this story thought Martinez and her crew couldn't do what they set out to do. They held onto stereotypes of who middle-aged women are and what they can do. What stereotypes do people have about teens and what they can do? Do *you* have stereotypes about categories of people?

When Martinez went on television to teach home repair, she didn't match the usual image of a woman her age. Do you see yourself in any of the teen characters on television or in movies? What, if anything, is accurate? What is not accurate at all?

When people assume you can't do something, what's your response?

When *you're* afraid you can't meet a new challenge, do you back down or go for it?

Vocabulary

You won't find the word "wommaned" in a dictionary because the writer made it up to fit the story—the traditional word would be "manned," which you can see would not make sense here. If you make up a word to make a point, remember to put quote marks around it to signal your reader that it was done on purpose.

Project possibilities

Interview three people who are over 50, and ask them what they might contribute to the well-being of the community, something that would surprise people. Are there ways you could assist them in making such contributions?

In what ways could you help change other people's mistaken images of teens?

An Unstoppable Dream

Imagine a dream so big that fire can't burn it, thieves can't steal it, and time can't weaken it. Then consider the story of **Samuel Hightower**.

A painting contractor, Hightower had the idea back in 1967 of a music school to give neighborhood kids a positive outlet for their energy and to help them stay off the streets and out of trouble. Inspired by his belief in kids' potential, he used his life savings to open a school in a Boston neighborhood where children were more likely to grow up with guns than guitars.

It wasn't hard getting volunteers to teach, or kids who wanted to learn. No child was turned away because of money. The school was popular, but within a year Dr. Martin Luther King, Jr. was assassinated. Because of the rioting that followed, the students and teachers could have been in danger in the building. "I didn't want anyone getting hurt because of me," he says.

He saved money for four years, bought a building in a safer place, and began fixing it up. But before the new school could open, it was vandalized, everything of value inside was stolen, and it was set on fire. Hightower couldn't afford repairs and eventually the city tore down the building. Once more all the money Hightower had put into his school, plus over a year of hard work, was gone. But he still wouldn't give up the dream.

"Every time I saw children on the street corner, I longed again to open the school," he says. And he did. In 1985, his program opened in a church basement, and right away there were more kids who wanted to learn than space to accommodate them. Hightower began raising money for a larger space and for instruments and transportation for pupils who couldn't afford either.

In the school, kids met weekly to master the basics of music theory before choosing an instrument and beginning the discipline of regular practice. Programs grew to include after-school activities with swimming, art, and music. He started a gospel choir, featuring singers as young as 11. Many adults volunteered to keep it all going.

What did all this mean to the kids? For one thing, they had a counterbalance to the streets. "Instead of selling drugs, they can practice the violin," says one of the volunteer teachers. "In this neighborhood, you have people who just grow into drugs."

Over the years, Hightower never stopped helping kids. At an age when most people have retired, Hightower was working to raise almost a million dollars to buy another building. He wants to remodel it for a 2,000 seat concert auditorium and a multicultural center.

Hightower's dream of helping kids through music has survived fire, riots, theft, and total financial losses. Why has he kept going? "When you're determined and really sincere, nothing can stop you," says Samuel Hightower.

To do

Comprehension & reflection

Sam Hightower is a painting contractor. Why do you think he chose to teach music instead of house painting? Do you think music was a good choice? Would it be a good choice in your neighborhood?

Research Martin Luther King, Jr. How did his life and his death affect our country? How was Sam Hightower's life affected by Dr. King's death?

How does the story show Hightower's determination? As you talk about the setbacks he faced, consider how you might have reacted to them. Why do Hightower's reactions make him a Giraffe Hero?

Vocabulary

How would you describe the difference between someone who wants to do something and someone who's *determined* to do something?

Draw a sketch in your journal to illustrate the word "counterbalance." Put negative peer pressure on one side of the balance, and what Sam Hightower brings to kids on the other side.

Project possibilities

Do you play an instrument? If so, could you teach someone else what you know about playing it?

If you were going to counterbalance negative peer pressure in your school, what steps could you take to do that?

If there are people in your community who are as committed to helping kids as Sam Hightower is, talk to them about the work they're doing and find out what help you might be able to offer.

Doing the Cans

While volunteering at a soup kitchen in New York, writer/actor **Guy Polhemus** talked with homeless people waiting for their food. He was surprised to discover how many of them tried to support themselves by redeeming cans and bottles. Unfortunately, store managers were giving them a hard time, limiting them to fewer than 50 containers a day or refusing to redeem them at all. Managers said that empties took up too much space, beverage distributors were too slow picking them up and paying the stores for them, and that the homeless were just too shabby to have hanging around.

The store managers weren't the only problem. If a consumer throws away a can or bottle instead of redeeming it, the beverage company that made it gets to keep the nickel deposit. Those nickels add up—to about $60 million a year for the companies, just in the New York area! They had no interest in making it easy to redeem those containers.

Polhemus was angry that the homeless were being treated badly when they tried to help themselves. Scavenging for containers was hard, dirty work. People who "do the cans" perform a useful service in clearing litter and in recycling resources. Polhemus felt they deserved their redemption money and a little common courtesy.

He channeled his anger in a useful direction by coming up with a plan for a nonprofit redemption center that would serve the homeless. "Everyone said it was an impossible plan—no money, no vacant lot, no building," Polhemus remembers.

Nevertheless he hopped on his bike and began pedaling up and down the city's streets looking for an empty space. He found a developer willing to let him use a midtown lot temporarily, rent-free. He borrowed money for a trailer and some equipment and We Can, the first redemption center for the poor and homeless, opened for business.

They flooded the muddy lot with 150,000 cans and bottles in the first ten weeks. At first many companies dragged their feet about coming to pick up the containers at We Can. Polhemus had to be relentlessly persistent, but he finally got the distributors to play fair. We Can was in business.

From the beginning Polhemus treated the people redeeming cans with fairness and dignity. He gave them vouchers that could be turned into cash at a nearby check-cashing store because he knew they liked getting a "paycheck" for their labors. In its first two years We Can wrote vouchers for $625,000 to redeemers, and as the operation grew, Polhemus hired homeless people to help run it. We Can also helped redeemers get legal and medical services.

Guy Polhemus says that We Can gave him a purpose in life. "The minute I took my focus off of my own problems—'poor me, a privileged, white-bread jerk'—and focused on reaching out to the needs around me, I discovered a deep sense of inner peace and conviction."

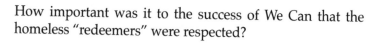

To do

Comprehension & reflection

What would it mean to a homeless person to discover We Can, to be greeted warmly and paid fairly, and eventually to earn himself a job there? How would that person's life be transformed?

Polhemus talks about developing a sense of "inner peace" through this work. What does that concept mean? Think of someone you know who shows a sense of inner peace. Describe that person and why you see him or her that way. Are there similarities between them? What are they?

How important was it to the success of We Can that the homeless "redeemers" were respected?

Vocabulary

This story is about redeeming cans and bottles, a very down-to-earth activity. "Redeem" and words that are made from that root—redeemer, redeeming, redemption—are more often used for matters of the spirit. How does the last line of the story relate to redeeming one man's spirit?

What is meant by the term "redeeming feature"? (Hint: It's not about cans *or* spirit.)

If you don't know the slang description, "white-bread," can you guess what Polhemus meant by it?

Project possibilities

In many states, there is no law requiring that a deposit be charged on containers, so people don't take empty cans or bottles back to stores. What are the benefits and the disadvantages of having a law requiring deposits? Is there a "deposit" law in your state? If there is not, and you think the benefits are strong, could you and your class advocate for such a law?

An alternative for dealing with cans and bottles is to recycle them. Are there recycling programs in your community? If there are, can you help get more people into the program? If there aren't, could you *start* a program?

The Good Steward

In her more than 20 years with the National Forest Service, **Gloria Flora** stood up for the environment again and again. Whether it was shutting down future oil and gas exploration in the Rocky Mountain Front or protecting threatened trout in Nevada, Flora, at age 44, was a veteran defender of public lands and resources. That's when she quit.

In a very public resignation from her job as supervisor of Nevada's Humboldt-Toiyabe National Forest, Flora sounded an alarm about the harassment of her staff by local anti-government citizens' groups and the lack of backup they were getting from the Service. She also accused Nevada's judicial system of being lax in prosecuting violators of environmental laws.

Flora's blast came as Forest Service employees and conservation advocates were confronted by anti-regulation Nevadans over the Service's refusal to rebuild a washed-out road into a wilderness area that was home to a threatened species of trout. Local politicians and a group calling themselves the Sagebrush Rebels organized protest marches and staged public meetings at which Flora witnessed public insults and threats against herself and her staff.

The "Rebels" dispatched a bulldozer to the washout site to reopen the road themselves. In local newspapers, Forest Service staffers were called "Nazis" and calls were made to harm them. They and their families were shunned throughout the community.

Flora's protests to the National Forest Service and to local law enforcement had produced no assistance for her embattled staff so she took the ultimate step to protect the nation's resources for future generations—she wrote that letter of protest and resignation. Forest Service Chief Mike Dombeck supported her claims, and later resigned himself over the directions being imposed on the Service.

Since her resignation, Flora has founded a nonprofit called Sustainable Obtainable Solutions (SOS), to promote sustainability on public lands. A frequent speaker on environmental issues, she reports that her host audiences are usually supportive, but she is sometimes harassed and threatened by "Fed-bashers" and has on occasion needed a police escort.

Does she regret taking on the anti-conservation forces? "There are risks that are external and some that are internal," says Gloria Flora. "The worst thing would be looking back on your life and thinking, 'That was *important*—I should have taken a stand.'"

To do

Comprehension & reflection

Flora's job with the Forest Service was to protect public lands. If you wanted to *use* those public lands, as the "Rebels" did, you might not be very happy with being told no. The conflict between private use and the Forest Service's duty has provoked controversy all over this country. See what you can find out about the conflicting viewpoints around the use of public lands. (Hint: they go back in history to the first establishment of federally protected areas.)

What does the concept of sustainability mean?

Name some things you think are worth sustaining in the world, in your community, or in your life. Why are these things important to you?

Vocabulary

What are the meanings of these prefixes: anti-, ex-, in-, pre-, pro-, con-, re-, com-, non- and em-? Understanding their meanings can increase your vocabulary enormously.

You might think all unfamiliar words are big ones, but how about the word "lax"? If it wasn't one of the words you looked up, look it up now.

Project possibilities

Go to *www.s-o-solutions.org* to see what Gloria Flora's organization is doing to foster sustainability.

Flora says, "the worst thing would be looking back on your life and thinking 'That was important—I should have taken a stand.'" Are there problems in your school or community that you might take a stand on?

The Choice of a Lifetime

John Croyle was a top defensive end for the University of Alabama's legendary coach, Bear Bryant. After Croyle's last game his teammates said, "See you in the pros." Croyle was that good. So did he (a) sign on as a pro football player for megabucks, or (b) go into debt to start a ranch for abused and abandoned kids?

Giraffe Hero John Croyle is the guy who picked (b). He started Big Oak Boys' Ranch with a wish, a prayer and some miraculously timely financial angels. Two days before Croyle had to come up with $45,000 to buy the ranch, a dentist from Birmingham arrived with $15,000 in hand. Then, with time really running out on the clock, a former 'Bama teammate donated the $30,000 signing bonus he'd just gotten from the New England Patriots. Croyle had his down payment.

Croyle started small, with five boys in the ranch's old four-room house. He had no experience with social workers, health inspectors or the juvenile justice system. When an official from the welfare department dropped in unexpectedly and asked to see his license, the obliging Croyle pulled out his *driver's* license. He didn't know he had to have a state license for housing kids.

The ranch grew to six large brick homes, each with houseparents caring for eight boys of various ages. It's a working ranch where the boys raise much of their food. Croyle's 6'7" frame is everywhere, helping with farm work and homework, or playing a fast game of basketball. He says, "They've never had anybody who trusted or depended on them. Now they do, and once somebody believes in you, half the battle is over."

Since 1975 more than a thousand boys have lived at the ranch, some for days and some for years. Croyle finds them in jails, hospitals, abusive homes and once, in a railroad boxcar. And he's started a similar ranch for girls.

Croyle promises new arrivals that he'll stick with them until they're grown. And if each new kid tries to be the best person he or she can be, they've got Croyle for life. When they graduate from school, Croyle helps them find jobs, get college scholarships or enlist in the services. He knows where most of his graduates are and what they're doing.

A local judge said, "If everybody had as much interest in their own children as John Croyle does in *any* kid, we wouldn't have delinquency in this country. It's that simple."

To do

Comprehension & reflection

John Croyle not only gave up serious money when he made his choice, he also gave up the chance of fame. Many people who make such choices talk about the emotional rewards of the work they choose to do. What might the emotional rewards be for Croyle's chosen work?

Athletes are often paid "megabucks." What other jobs earn enormous salaries? Use the Internet or the library to learn what various jobs pay. Do you agree with the numbers as they are, or would you change them if you were in charge? What jobs do you think should earn the most? Which ones the least? What are the reasons for your choices?

If you talk about these things in class, remember to be a respectful listener. You may not agree with classmates' ideas, and they may not agree with yours. But everyone deserves to be heard, with no putdowns.

Vocabulary

Have you been remembering to do the exercises below?

Find any words in this story that are not completely familiar to you. See if you can understand their meanings by the way they're used in the story. Then look them up in a dictionary and put them in your vocabulary notebook, with a brief definition of each one. Use each word in a sentence that you make up yourself.

There are compound words in this story. Look at the story again and find at least three of them.

Project possibilities

Learn more about how Big Oak works at *www.bigoak.org*.

John Croyle has dedicated his life to helping young people have better lives. What might you or your class do to help kids who need someone to take an interest in them?

A Champion for the Children

When he was 12, **Craig Kielburger** read about the murder of a Pakistani child named Iqbal, who had escaped from slavery and had spoken out about the persistence of this nightmare. Both the murder and the idea that there were children like Iqbal shocked the young Canadian reader. He didn't intend to start a global movement, but he knew he had to do *something*.

What he did was found Free the Children, a nonprofit youth organization dedicated to ending the exploitation of children's labor worldwide.

"What this is all about is political will," he explained. "If our own country and other countries made it clear that child labor is both illegal and unacceptable, then this problem wouldn't exist."

Craig set out to create that political will, embarking on a fact-finding trip through five Asian countries, and attracting major media coverage all along the way. People were fascinated that a child was taking on this enormous issue.

He presented his findings to a US Congressional committee and met with the US Vice President and with representatives of the International Labor Organization at United Nations. He went to Geneva, Switzerland, for a World Council of Churches meeting, where he urged the churches to take on this international problem. Everywhere he went, people agreed to help Kielburger free the children.

Today the organization started by one deeply concerned 12-year-old has built more than 350 rural schools for kids in poor countries, kids who might otherwise never be literate. These children are not chained to rug looms, as the murdered Pakistani boy was, working 14 hours a day for no pay.

Kielburger has visited over 40 countries to speak out for children's rights. He's met with Presidents and Prime Ministers, heads of major corporations, the Pope, the Queen of England, the Dalai Lama and the late Mother Teresa.

The thousands of kids and adults who have joined Free the Children have helped fund the distribution of 3.5 million dollars worth of medical supplies for needy families. The organization is now supporting clean-water projects, health clinics, and economic cooperatives as well as schools in 21 non-industrial nations. All the actions they take help make life better for families so children do not have to go to work.

Kielburger is proud that so much of the support for the movement is from other kids.

"We're capable of doing more than watching television, playing video games, or hanging around malls," says Craig Kielburger. "Young people have the power to make a positive contribution to this world. I won't give up until the exploitation of all children has ended and all children have their rights."

To do

Comprehension & reflection

Kielburger believes kids are capable of stopping child slavery in the world. What do you think of his approach and his hopes?

The murdered child whose story inspired Craig Kielburger was sold to a carpet manufacturer for the equivalent of $12—his family had no other way to pay a debt they owed to a money lender. How can Free the Children's work in improving life for poor families help end such sales of children?

What is meant by "children's rights"? What other rights movements do you know about? What are the similarities and differences among them? What does the Bill of Rights say are the rights of all citizens in our country?

Use the Internet or the library to find out about child labor. When was it declared illegal in this country? In what countries is it still allowed?

What differences might there be between jobs that are OK for children to do and those that are exploitation? (Hint: If you're asked to do chores at home, that doesn't mean you're being exploited.)

Vocabulary

"Political will" is a term that does not refer to the political *parties*. Research the meaning of the term.

What does the term "media coverage" mean?

What's the difference between the word "speaking" and the term "speaking out"?

How does the prefix "non-" change the meaning of a word?

Project possibilities

How can your actions affect child labor abusers around the world? Who makes the products you buy and use? How would you find out? If something you want to buy had been made by a child, would you still buy it? What would happen if you did *not* buy it and told the seller your reason?

Are there any projects at *www.freethechildren.org* that inspire you to get involved?

The Art of Healing Lives

Can a paintbrush mend a broken heart? Yes, if it's in the hands of a homeless boy or girl who's using it to express sadness, rage, and the fear caused by having nowhere to go. Yes, when it helps a child go from withdrawn and isolated to hopeful and trusting. Yes, if **Gloria Simoneaux** is involved.

Simoneaux is the teacher, counselor, and artist who founded DrawBridge, a nonprofit organization in the San Francisco area. She explains that children in the program use art to "combat the despair of homelessness. Their pictures act as a bridge between their hidden inner world and those who care about them," says Simoneaux.

When parents are struggling to keep a family alive, it's hard for them to think about things beyond food and shelter. Simoneaux's work feeds the children's spirits. She recalls a child who "rarely spoke," but poured out his feelings when he talked about his paintings. "When you draw your feelings, people can't misunderstand you," says another youngster in a DrawBridge program.

Simoneaux got the idea for DrawBridge after years of making art with seriously ill children in hospitals. She convinced a homeless shelter to let her paint with the kids there for a few hours a week. "The first day," she says, "I knew I was in the right place."

Simoneaux worked full time for no pay until she began getting some grants that allowed her to take a small salary. She used her own modest resources to launch DrawBridge and says that getting money for the program is still a constant struggle.

A single mom with two children, she's also endured criticism for devoting any of her time and resources to other people's kids. But Simoneaux's love for her own children has fueled her work with homeless kids. "These children were beautiful, talented, and intelligent—absolutely no different from my own kids. And, the images they created were filled with deep pain, fear and loneliness."

Simoneaux boosts the kids' self-esteem by helping them assist others in need. She says that the kids were amazed when sales of their art and crafts generated $5,000 for homeless hurricane victims in Latin America.

Simoneaux attacks the effects of homelessness on many different fronts. Because so many homeless students struggle and even fail in school, she started a program to sensitize teachers and other students to the challenges that homeless students face. Formerly homeless teens deliver the presentation, which features DrawBridge art and a video that helps viewers separate fact from fiction about homelessness.

While families look for permanent housing, DrawBridge offers not only art programs but also therapy referrals, help in getting after-school jobs and stays in summer camps. Once families secure housing, their kids often keep coming to DrawBridge programs, sometimes becoming DrawBridge counselors. Simoneaux has helped gifted DrawBridge students earn scholarships.

Always seeking to raise awareness about homelessness, Simoneaux created a traveling art show called "Through Our Eyes" that features 148 pieces of art by DrawBridge students. She also publishes a newsletter that showcases the kids' art and stories, and greeting cards featuring the kids' art. The sales turn into royalties for the young artists. "We were able to give one child an $800 check," Simoneaux says proudly.

From that first visit Simoneaux made to a shelter, DrawBridge has grown to serve 1,500 children in 19 shelters. She supervises a staff of 30 volunteers and 12 counselors and is training people to start similar efforts in other cities.

Although she's spent long hours and earned little money, Gloria Simoneaux doesn't focus on what this work has cost her. She simply says, "I feel privileged to be working with the children."

To do

Comprehension & reflection

In this story, as in so many others in this book, a hero believes in shared humanity and acts on that belief. Simoneaux sees that homeless children are just like her own kids. What other stories in this book involve seeing the similarities among people?

How is your world affected if you look at people and see the ways in which they are like you, rather than what's different about them?

Take that thought to a larger scale and consider the ways that seeing differences rather than similarities affects social and political events.

If you agree that making art is a good way to express feelings, then create a poem, drawing, dance or song that expresses yours.

Vocabulary

Find any words in this story that are not completely familiar to you. See if you can understand their meanings by the way they're used in the story. Then look them up in a dictionary and put them in your vocabulary notebook, with a brief definition of each one. Use each word in a sentence that you make up yourself.

This story uses many words that describe emotions such as sadness, rage, fear, despair and loneliness. The children in the story use art rather than words to express these emotions. When you want to communicate your feelings, do you use words? What words are in your emotional vocabulary? (Hint: "I feel......., ... and ...." Fill in the blanks.)

Project possibilities

There are, in all our lives, people who view each other with suspicion because they're "different." Are there individuals or groups in your life who might be persuaded to become less suspicious? One effective way to do that is to get them working together on a project, especially if that project involves doing service for others.

Are there sick or homeless children in your community who could use a DrawBridge program? Go to *www.drawbridge. org* and see how Simoneaux does her work.

Homesteading in the City

The word "homesteader" may make you think of covered wagons, log cabins and wheat fields. But **Louise Stanley** led people to become homesteaders in burnt-out tenements and abandoned apartments in a tough part of Brooklyn, New York, a long way from any wheat fields.

The section of Brooklyn called East New York used to be a good place to live. Back in 1967, Louise Stanley, a postal worker, was happy to buy a house there. It was a good place to raise her six children.

But the area began to deteriorate and, after years of neglect, many buildings had been abandoned. Because the buildings' owners were not paying taxes on these properties, the city officially owned them and had put padlocks on the doors. Some buildings were torched. Vacant lots had turned into trash heaps. Dealers and addicts were breaking into empty buildings.

In a city where good affordable housing is practically a myth, Louise Stanley hated seeing all the once fine buildings standing empty or seized by criminals.

Stanley attended a meeting of ACORN, the Association of Community Organizations for Reform Now, a group that organizes low-income and moderate-income families, helping them get good housing and good jobs.

She had come to the meeting just to listen, but she soon found herself raising her hand, speaking her mind, and then volunteering to work on the housing problem. She agreed to lead neighbors who shared her concerns in the first East New York ACORN group.

Stanley and her ACORN group organized people to reclaim and renovate abandoned buildings in their neighborhood. Stanley and her team helped families break the padlocks on city-owned buildings and move in. With ACORN's volunteers, the new residents started repairing them, making them again good places to raise families. Neighbors provided these urban homesteaders with electricity and water.

The city government ordered the new residents arrested for trespassing. Stanley was *pleased*. She alerted the press. People all over Brooklyn and the other parts of New York City were shocked by news stories about the city arresting poor families who needed housing and were willing to work hard to repair these old places. If the city was just locking the buildings, and these people were willing to fix them up, this was a good thing, not a reason to arrest them. People thought the drug dealers should be arrested, not these hard-working families.

City official were embarrassed by the stories and began to negotiate with Stanley to solve the problem. They struck a deal: Stanley agreed that ACORN would not break into any more buildings. And the city agreed to start giving abandoned housing units to community groups for renovation. The city also provided $2.7 million to buy renovation materials for 58 buildings!

Not a bad result for a novice organizer. Louise Stanley says, "The bottom line is getting people to realize that success is possible." Even when that means making really big changes in attitudes and policies.

 To do

Comprehension & reflection

As you learned when you researched Martin Luther King, Jr. and Mohandas Gandhi, they were heroes who practiced civil disobedience. They worked for changes in unjust laws, and when it was necessary, they deliberately and peacefully broke those laws, accepting the consequence of being jailed. In going to prison, they brought attention to their causes, and the resulting changes in public opinion led to the changing of the laws. How does Louise Stanley's story relate to what those heroes did? Review the stories of Doris Haddock and Hazel Wolf for other peaceful acts of civil disobedience.

Vocabulary

"The bottom line" is an expression from the business world meaning the ultimate financial results of a company's work. It has moved into the language to mean the final outcome of any endeavor. What other expressions can you think of that have made the leap from a limited meaning to a larger one? (Hint: there are hundreds of common expressions that began in sports and now have wider meanings.)

What meaning do you see in the acronym ACORN?

Project possibilities

See how ACORN works at *www.acorn.org*.

If there are resources in your community that have been abandoned, perhaps a neglected park or an old activities center, is there something you or your class could do to make it useful again?

A Cocoon for Throwaway Kids

Sarri Gilman will tell you, "We recycle cans better than these kids are treated." To Gilman, a social worker in Everett, Washington, "these kids" are the nation's homeless teenagers. She'll tell you about the 14-year-old girl with the six-month-old baby, neither of whom had slept in three days. Or Marcus, whose mom is dead and whose father is in jail. Or Lena, 16, abandoned by her mom at age six and left with an alcoholic father who abused her. Some experts say that on any given night, there are half a million such teenagers on the nation's streets.

Unlike many people who see homeless teens, Gilman didn't look the other way. For years she had worked with at-risk adolescents and knew how serious teen homelessness was in her community. She says, "I got tired of seeing the pain behind the eyes of these youngsters. ... It kept me awake at night trying to figure out what I could do to make a difference."

That "difference" became a miracle known as Cocoon House, a safe haven for teenagers in crisis. It's a beautiful home that shelters teens for a night, a week, or even a few months, while they get help locating a stable home. At Cocoon House, teens find safety, warmth, clean beds and clothes, toiletries, a living room, and a big yard. There's also a dinner table where kids eat together as a family, a first-time experience for some of them.

This cocoon was not spun overnight. When Gilman started, she had no track record, no money, and was unknown in the community. Friends warned her she'd go bankrupt. When she asked civic leaders for assistance, some of them denied there was a problem. She was criticized for being "too optimistic," for having expectations of kids that were too high. But Gilman persisted—she was on a mission.

Gilman persuaded the local Lions Club to buy the building that would become Cocoon House. She enlisted innumerable volunteers to help fix it up. She spent countless hours reaching out to businesses and social service agencies. The harder Gilman worked, the more the community responded. But even with increasing support, when the doors opened, Cocoon House had just $15 in the bank.

Gilman never backed down, and Cocoon House not only survived its modest beginning, it grew. And Gilman went right on to build Cocoon Complex, a converted motel that today houses two dozen young people who can stay for up to three years, many of them working in a nonprofit restaurant that the kids run themselves while they finish school, save money and—most important—heal.

Hundreds of Cocoon kids have moved on to stable housing, to diplomas or GEDs, and then to jobs. Recently Cocoon House heard from a former resident who's employed by a software company and sharing a house with friends. He ended his letter with, "Sarri, thank you for believing in me, and for opening your heart to so many others whose lives would be wasted without the dream that you made happen."

To do

Comprehension & reflection

Storytelling is a traditional way of getting people to understand a point. How do the stories of Cocoon House kids make it clear that Sarri Gilman's work is important? Consider the power of storytelling when you have a point you want to make—people forget facts and figures, but they remember stories.

What does it mean to have a mission? Do you know someone who has a mission? What affect does it have on their actions?

Vocabulary

Sometimes a word is used in a way that gives it new meaning. Apply the word "recycle" to Sarri Gilman's work with homeless teens.

Combining the words "social" and "worker" creates a job title. What does a social worker normally do?

What does it mean to "back down"? How does it differ from to "back up"?

Do you think that "cocoon" is a good description for this kind of homeless shelter? Why or why not?

Project possibilities

See what's new at cocoon house at *www.cocoonhouse.org*. Does it give you any good ideas?

Are there homeless kids in *your* community? If there are, what's being done to help "recycle" them back into safe homes? Is there any way you can assist such efforts?

Of all the problem-solving that could be done in your world, do you see one thing that might become a mission for you?

Azim Khamisa and Ples Felix, holding their boys' pictures.

The Power of Forgiveness

The bare facts of the story are these: **Azim Khamisa's** son, Tariq, was making a delivery for a San Diego pizza parlor when he was shot and killed in a failed robbery attempt by a gang. The killer was **Ples Felix's** 14-year-old grandson and ward, Tony Hicks, who was sentenced as an adult for the murder and is now imprisoned.

That could have been the end of the story. But it was only the beginning, as you might guess from the photo above. That's Khamisa on the left, Felix on the right.

Khamisa, a banker whose family had fled violence in East Africa years earlier, was devastated by his son's death, yet he reached out to the killer's family, realizing that they too had lost a boy.

Felix, a former Green Beret who is a program manager for San Diego County, was devastated by what his grandson had done—on the first night he had ever defied his grandfather and left the house to meet with the gang. Felix went alone to a gathering of the grieving Khamisa family, telling them of his own grief over his grandson's deed.

Khamisa established a foundation in his son's memory, and he and Felix formed an alliance that transforms their losses into a resolve to see that other families do not suffer such tragedies.

"There were victims on both ends of the gun," says Khamisa. "Ples and I have become like brothers."

The two men developed an anti-violence program that they take again and again into schools—together. They talk to students about Tariq's death and about Tony's imprisonment. They talk about gangs, they help the kids talk about the awful effects of violence on their own lives, and they help them affirm that they will avoid violence themselves.

Kids hearing the two men's story and seeing them working together also get an unforgettable picture of a response to violence that is not more violence and hatred.

Commenting on their work together, Khamisa says, "Every time you talk one youngster out of committing homicide, you save two."

Both Felix and Khamisa are speaking out for "restorative justice," a way of dealing with criminals that helps lawbreakers understand what they have done and make restitution to those they have harmed, rather than just sending them to prisons. "The way we deal now with lawbreakers does nothing for those they have injured, for reforming the criminal or for repairing society," says Ples Felix.

He and Khamisa are helping Tony Hicks learn and grow while he's in prison. When he's freed, they hope he'll work with them at the Tariq Khamisa Foundation, helping other kids avoid the tragedy of violence.

To do

Comprehension & reflection

Felix and Khamisa formed an alliance to stop kids from killing kids. Do you see the power of their working together when people expect them to be enemies?

What does Khamisa mean when he says, "There were victims on both ends of the gun?"

Why do you think the word "devastated" was used to describe both men?

If there are people in your life who have harmed you, do you feel you must do them equal harm? Why or why not?

Consider the long-standing conflicts among nations around the world and the role that revenge plays in the fighting. How might the world be changed if people who have been harmed were able to forgive rather than seek revenge?

Using the Internet or the library, learn about restorative justice. When you have more information, consider your opinion of the concept. How would it change our justice system? Do you think such changes would be good ones? Why or why not?

Vocabulary

What words in this story were made by putting two complete words together? As you know, these are compound words.

What words in the story have prefixes? Consider the word "form." How is its meaning changed by the prefix "re"? How is it changed by the prefix "trans"?

The phrase "dealing with" is used in this story. How is the meaning of "dealing" changed by pairing it with the word "with"?

Project possibilities
Get an update on the work that Khamisa and Felix are doing, at *www.tkf.org*.

What alliances do you have in your life? (Hint: friendships count when they involve working together for a shared goal. Families can be alliances, if the family members are all pulling together for a purpose.)

Are there alliances in your community? What are their goals? If there's something you'd like to get done in your school or community, are there alliances you could make with others who would like to work on the same goal?

From Pretend Hero to Real

"Winston Man" **David Goerlitz** used to make $75,000 a year from just one of his many modeling contracts; he was the Winston Man, the square-jawed hero of a cigarette advertising campaign that depicted him as a smoke jumper, a search-and-rescue team member and other "soldiers of fortune," all puffing away. He was a live version of the G.I. Joe action figure. Goerlitz himself smoked more than three packs a day. Though he had health problems that doctors blamed on his heavy smoking, he wouldn't quit.

Then he visited his brother in a Boston hospital. "There's nothing more gut-wrenching than the Winston Man walking around a cancer hospital—pompous, arrogant… not believing the doctors telling me that people are dying in the lung cancer wards, and all of them smoked. That was face-to-face reality that I never saw before, or if I saw it, I denied it."

Goerlitz quit smoking. The contract he had signed promising not to criticize the product had expired just the month before.

Goerlitz embarked on a campaign to stop the industry's targeting of 11-to-14-year-old kids. He knows that 75% of all smokers start before the age of 14; the tobacco companies know it too. Images such as the Winston Man are specifically designed to appeal to young people who want to look older, cooler, and in control. A marketing executive told Goerlitz that Winston had dropped its previous "construction worker" ad campaign because the agency said, "kids don't want to be construction workers any more; they want to be heroes."

Goerlitz has facts and figures to back up his assertion that our society in general and our government in particular have tacitly endorsed this threat to kids' health. He's appalled that the #1 addictive drug in America is not regulated by the FDA, that 50 chemicals labeled "zero tolerance" by the EPA in any other form are allowed in cigarettes, and that $3 billion is spent per year to advertise a product with absolutely no positive value.

Goerlitz says he himself was fat, cross-eyed and ugly at age 14. He started smoking because he thought he'd get confidence from cigarettes. "I wanted to be everything the ads showed." Now he's trying to make up for being the image that headed other kids toward this addiction. He says he wants to move from "being an ad model to being a role model."

In order to do this, Goerlitz sacrificed his lucrative modeling career. The conglomerates that sell tobacco also own thousands of other major companies, none of them likely to want the services of David Goerlitz. Goerlitz told us, "I don't blame them. People say, 'What if he sold milk and gets fat around his heart,'… People are afraid of what I might do."

Goerlitz supports his family with residuals (ongoing payments for past work), income from a small acting school he runs, and the occasional modeling assignment from a brave sponsor. Most of his time is spent crisscrossing the country educating students about the dangers of tobacco. He's also testified before a Congressional committee, pushing for legislation that would ban all image advertising by cigarette companies.

Goerlitz approaches his no-smoking campaign with all the verve and style he once brought to being the Winston Man. But he's not looking for any pats on the back—he's doing this for the kids who bought his nicotine number.

To do

Comprehension & reflection

In cigarette ads, Goerlitz had the image of an adventure "hero," and he was always smoking. The image paired being a hero and being a smoker. Pay close attention to the ads and commercials you see. What images do you see being used to sell products now? What pairing do you see? (Hint: tooth paste + popularity would be an example.)

This story talks about giving kids advertising images that are attractive. Do you think it's a good thing to advertise to young kids? To teens? Why or why not?

Goerlitz talks about tacitly endorsing a threat to kids' health. Are there negative things that you tacitly endorse?

Vocabulary

You can often figure out the meanings of words by connecting thoughts in the story. These are "context clues." Read the first sentence about this Giraffe Hero. Now tie those words to these: Goerlitz sacrificed his lucrative modeling career. The context gives you a sense of what "lucrative" means.

Sometimes a reader gets lucky and an unfamiliar word

is defined immediately by the author. Find the word "residual" in the story and read the parenthetic explanation that follows it. It's fine to have this explanation, but there are *other* meanings for this word, so look it up—even though its meaning here is clear.

Project possibilities

Get updates on what David Goerlitz is doing about tobacco advertising at *www.davidgoerlitz.com*.

Goerlitz decided to work for a new law that would ban image advertising by tobacco companies. Ask your Social Studies teacher for information on how the process works to get new laws passed.

Are there changes in legislation that you think would be a good idea? Many people do what Goerlitz has done—urging legislators to make important changes in the laws. Find out what new laws are being considered in your community. Do any of them interest you enough to work for or against their becoming laws?

Are there new laws you'd like to propose, or old laws you'd like to see repealed? Students who learn their issue well and make persuasive presentations to law-makers *have* achieved legislative changes. For just two examples, check out the Discovery School at *www.giraffe.org/discovery* and the SWaMP Kids in this book on page 82.

Rolling for Reading

Toni Cordell-Seipel has traveled the world filming television shows. She's been charged by an angry water buffalo, searched by gun-toting soldiers, and attacked by a snake charmer's cobra. But nothing ever scared her as much as the fear that someone would discover that she could barely read. Cordell-Seipel kept her secret for 35 years.

When she was a kid, other students called her a dummy, and teachers treated her as if she just wasn't trying. She knows now that she should have gotten help for her problem. Instead she just got angry. Being a poor reader just made everything so difficult for her.

When she grew up, her own children couldn't understand why she never read them storybooks or helped with their homework. Only Cordell-Seipel knew that by the time her son was in fifth grade he could read better than she could. She had to read a paragraph three times before it made any sense to her.

She thought it was too late to do anything about her problem, but she changed her mind after seeing a movie about a grown man who admitted his illiteracy and learned to read.

At age 45, Toni Cordell-Seipel signed up for adult reading lessons. Within a year she was teaching other people. She was so happy to be literate that she wanted to do something to let other non-reading adults know they weren't too old to learn either.

Because she's media savvy, she knew it had to be something unusual so that newspapers and TV stations would notice and cover the story. Her answer was to start rolling for reading. First she roller-skated across her home state of Oklahoma talking to students and community groups along the way. That trip brought a lot of attention to the problem of illiteracy, so she began to plan something bigger—she decided to become the first women to roller-skate across the US. She put her skates on in San Gabriel, California, and rolled into Jacksonville, Florida, five months and 2,300 miles later.

She skated 15-30 miles a day, and gave talks in the towns she passed through. It was hard work physically and the costs of the trip ate up the family savings, but she got a tremendous boost from knowing she was getting kids and adults fired up about reading.

At one school an eleven-year-old boy stood up in a crowded auditorium and told her, "I'm just like you. The kids make fun of me. They tell me I'm stupid." She spoke to him right from her heart. "I think you're one of the bravest people I ever met. You've just proven that you're not afraid of what people think of you. Just because other people call us names doesn't mean they're right." She told him, "If you're not learning the way the information is presented, it doesn't mean you're lazy or stupid. It simply means you need to be taught a different way."

Toni Cordell-Seipel knew how illiteracy could make you feel like an outsider, but she also knew that everyone could learn. That's why she stuck her neck out to go public with the secret she had kept so long.

Comprehension & reflection

Imagine you're an adult shooting footage all over the world for television programs. You have to follow directions for getting places, understand messages and questions that are sent to you, and write reports on what you've done. No one at work or at home knows you read like a little kid, and you have to be sure they don't find out. How are your work and home life affected?

Have you ever skated a mile? What would it feel like to skate 30 miles in a day? Given the physical hardship of the task, what do you think of Cordell-Seipel's commitment to adult literacy?

If reading is difficult for you, have you told your teachers and your family that you're having trouble?

Vocabulary

A thesaurus gives you not the dictionary meanings for words, but other words that you might use as alternatives to the one you're looking up. Choose two words from this story and use a thesaurus to find other words that have similar meanings. For example, you could find other words to use instead of savvy, literate, admitted, community, or stupid.

Project possibilities

You can get new information about teaching literacy at *www.literacynet.org/value*. Toni Cordell-Seipel founded this nonprofit group after completing her cross-country skate.

If reading is easy for you, is there someone you could help who's having a hard time learning?

Many causes sponsor walks, runs or bicycle events to raise money for their work. Is there a cause you care enough about to enter one of these fundraising events?

Are there adult literacy classes in your community? If there are, can you assist in any way? If not, would you be interested in helping get a program started?

Turning Pity into Respect

Pretend you're on a sea-going expedition that's so dangerous nobody's ever done it before. You, the leader, have one leg. Your crew is three teenaged boys, each missing a limb, plus a 23-year-old blind man. And you make history—you're the first people ever to complete the perilous journey.

You are a teacher of children with disabilities, many of them orphans. You train boys with missing fingers to be mechanics, young men with only one arm to be fishers. Your *other* leg is amputated, and you go right on.

Welcome to the incredible world of combat veteran, sailor, adventurer, writer, and teacher, **Tristan Jones**.

Jones survived three wartime sinkings and was badly injured by an explosion. He held nine world sailing records, most of them for crossing the Atlantic Ocean solo. He sailed further up the Amazon than anyone before him ever had. He wrote 17 books and over 300 articles and short stories. But of all his challenges, the one he fought hardest was conquering prejudice against people with disabilities.

Jones' left leg was amputated at the thigh after his war injury and before most of his record-breaking sailing adventures, one of which took him to 34 countries on five continents. When he got to Thailand he stayed, seeing that life was terribly hard for people with disabilities there, especially children. Disabilities, in many countries, mean being shamed and either kept out of sight or sent out to beg.

Jones taught dozens of disabled boys to support themselves, as fishers, sailors and mechanics. Four of them joined Jones on the grueling expedition across the treacherous Isthmus of Kra in Thailand, the journey that had never been done before—and has not even been attempted by anyone since. Jones reported triumphantly, "We five cripples succeeded where armies and navies had previously failed." The story is now told in Thailand's schools, showing the remarkable spirit of young people once shunned as helpless and hopeless outcasts.

A few years later Jones' other leg was amputated. Some people might have sunk into self-pity, but Jones continued to sail, write, teach, and work with disabled children. As he taught them skills and pride, he also appealed to the entire world, writing, "I plead for a change of social attitudes toward the disabled. I want to show the world that disabled people can accomplish almost anything they set their hearts on."

Tristan Jones knew that the results of his work would be visible long after his own death. He said, "If in your travels you ever come across a one-legged or one-armed Thai seaman who looks you straight in the eye, who is not ashamed of his deformity, you'll know he was one of my boys."

 **To do**

Comprehension & reflection
Tristan Jones was a physical "action" hero before he became a social activist, advocating for all people with disabilities. How did he use his physical skills and bravery to achieve his advocacy work?

In a place where you're reasonably safe, blindfold yourself and move from one place to another, perhaps from your bed to the kitchen. How does it feel to lose your sense of sight?

Put one hand in a pocket and don't use it for an hour, no matter what task you have to do in that time. How does it change your actions to not have the use of one hand?

Are you a different person without your sight, or without the use of one of your hands? If these things were truly lost to you, how would you want others to treat you?

If you could go on an expedition, where would you want to go? Why?

Vocabulary
How does the prefix "dis-" affect the meaning of the word "abilities"?

Language used to describe other people is often gentler than the words they may use to describe themselves. What words did Jones use to describe disabilities and the people who have them? Many people with disabilities would be deeply offended if people who do *not* have disabilities used these words.

Project possibilities

Are there groups in your community working on disability issues? Are there organizations speaking up? If this issue interests you, how might you help?

Do you know a student or faculty member who has a disability? Invite them to class to talk about the services available in your community, and what helpful services might be missing.

Facing Down the Racists

"Racism? What's that?" **Sandy Dore** hopes that someday people will ask this question. Until then, he'll be fighting against racism in all its forms.

For over 25 years, Dore has been a teacher, counselor and activist in Kelowna, British Columbia, a small community in Canada, near the US border. A few years ago it was chosen by white supremacists as a place to spread their message of hatred and intolerance towards Jews and people of color. Supremacists often target areas where they believe there will be little resistance to their efforts. When they guessed that Kelowna would be such a community, they were wrong.

As soon as hate literature and racist graffiti started appearing there, Dore knew he had to act, especially when the hate campaign zeroed in on his own school. "Communities get apathetic if something doesn't galvanize them," says Dore.

Many in the community were indeed apathetic; even some fellow teachers dismissed the matter as unimportant. Others cautioned him not to "rock the boat." Undaunted, Dore organized three groups to spread human rights education throughout the district. Thanks to his work, many schools committed to policies of respect for others regardless of race, creed or color. Dore and his allies created pro-diversity T-shirts and posters, and even convinced the city government to proclaim Kelowna a racism-free town. Eventually, most of the white supremacist organizers got the message and left.

Dore then turned the tables on the supremacists and took the anti-racist battle into places where they thought they were strong. He was part of an educational symposium on Holocaust survivors. "Holocaust" refers to the deliberate attempt of the Nazis to kill all the Jews in Europe during World War II. They succeeded in killing millions, but there are people today who deny it ever happened. Dore says this denial is "very disturbing and *must* be challenged at every opportunity." When the symposium was given in communities where supremacists believed they had a stronghold, packed audiences gave overwhelming support to the anti-racist message.

Dore's activism has put him in considerable danger. He and his family have been the targets of threatening phone calls and mail. Once when he traveled to give a lecture, the local police had to put a guard outside his hotel room. He's had police escorts to his speeches. A local official advised Dore to wear a bulletproof vest when he spoke.

In spite of the dangers, Dore hasn't slowed down or backed off. He says that "teachers should be the guys that are leading—we should be standing up there and saying what we believe." Expect Sandy Dore to keep standing up until racism is a thing of the past.

To do

Comprehension & reflection

Sandy Dore's actions to stop racism have brought him threats of physical harm. Consider the concept of solving disagreements without threats or actual violence. How would this work in Dore's world? In the world at large?

How could apathy increase racism? Research the Holocaust and consider the ways apathy helped make it possible for the Nazis to kill so many people.

When terrible things are happening, what is the responsibility of the people who know what's going on?

If you or someone you know has been affected by racism, consider what happened, what harm was done and how the situation might have been changed.

Vocabulary

Find at least three compound words in this story—the words created by making two words into one.

There are also many words in the story that are made of a word with a prefix, such as in-, un-, pro-, or anti-. Some words have *suffixes* such as -less, or –free. Take a word, any word, and see if you can make other words out of it by adding prefixes or suffixes.

Project possibilities

What would happen if you and your classmates took a stand against racism? Can you declare your classroom racism-free? How about your school? What would you have to do to make that happen?

As an individual, what actions could you take that would lessen racism in your world? (Hint: you could stand up for someone who's being harassed for being "different," even if it's not a matter of race. Maybe the harassment is about dressing "wrong," or having unpopular views.) Understanding that being different is not a reason for cruelty is a small but important step toward preventing huge crimes like the Holocaust.

The SWaMP Kids with their teacher, Alice Terry. Photo by Johnny Crawford

Talkin' Trash

They call em the SWaMP Kids
And they're always talkin' trash!
They freaked out the grown-ups
But they save em tons of cash!

A mountain of garbage
County didn't have a clue,
The clock was a-tickin'
Till those SWaMP Kids came through!

Don't be concerned if you never heard of a group called the **SWaMP Kids**, because they weren't a band—they were a dozen seventh graders in Franklin County, Georgia, whose "trash talk" was about reducing it, recycling it, and managing it.

Garbage isn't glamorous and dumps aren't dazzling, but they're huge problems in our country. Americans throw away a lot of stuff—if one year's worth of our trash got hauled to a dump in a single trip, it would take a convoy of ten-ton trucks 145,000 miles long!

Each year there's more waste but less space to put it in. That's why many states, including Georgia, have ordered local governments to create Solid Waste Management Plans (SWaMPs) to deal responsibly with local garbage.

The SWaMP Kids, as they came to be known, got their start with an Earth Day project. Teacher Alice Terry's students were promoting a first-ever recycling program for their county. They created a skit called "Recyclerella" to educate students and the public about the three R's—Reducing, Reusing and Recycling.

When they studied the whole issue of waste management, they discovered that their county didn't have the comprehensive waste management plan required by Georgia law. What's more, the county had no plan to start one, and was about to face a $10,000 *per day* fine for having no plan. They also faced big expenses for hauling the county's trash to a distant dump—the local dump was close to full.

The kids decided that *they* could write a plan, even though it meant they'd have to sacrifice their after-school time and to step outside the safety of the classroom and into a new world of government offices and county board meetings, all filled with disbelieving adults. "They had to contact legislators about laws and call various agencies about guidelines, so it was much more than just caring about the topic," says Terry.

The SWaMP Kids began asking for meetings with county officials. The hardest thing was getting adults to take them seriously. The officials couldn't believe that seventh graders could do the job. Then the kids spoke at a public meeting, and it was obvious to everyone there that these seventh graders knew more about making such a plan than anyone else in the room. The kids got official approval to write the county's plan, a job that other counties had paid adult consultants up to $20,000 to do. The SWaMP kids didn't ask to be paid; they just wanted to help their community.

The kids had a goal: though the dump had been declared almost full, they would make a plan that would keep it open for 10 years by reducing the amount of trash that went into it, mainly by recycling. The kids wrote budgets, studied land limitations, and even got the five towns in the county to cooperate with each other, something they didn't usually do.

The result was a 756-page plan that saved the county huge fines, a big consulting fee, distance hauling fees and, most importantly, extended the life of the dump by at least 20 years. It was the only such plan in the state.

How did kids succeed where adults were failing? "What's valuable about a group of kids is that they tackle a project with a different perspective," says Terry. The SWaMP Kids' story is told in schools across America to show what amazing things kids can accomplish when they stick their necks out and become active citizens of their community.

To do

Comprehension & reflection

Imagine working with 11 other students to write a 756-page paper on how to save a dump. What do you think had to be in the plan?

There's a stereotype in this story that these seventh-graders had to overcome. What was the stereotype and how do you think it was affected by the work that they did?

Vocabulary

The term "waste management" refers to dealing with all the trash and garbage people produce. What are *all* the meanings of the word "waste"?

What does it mean to be comprehensive? How does it relate to "comprehension"?

Project possibilities

Find out about the waste management plan for your own community. Does it include reducing, reusing and recycling? (Note the alliteration there.) If it doesn't, how long will it be before the plan no longer works? Is there a way you can encourage the community to throw fewer things away?

Being a citizen means something, even when you're not old enough to vote. The SWaMP Kids were active citizens of their community because they found a way to contribute. What can you do to be an active citizen and make your community a better place?

A Teenaged Whirlwind

If you ask some teens what they're doing, they're likely to answer—"Nothing." If you ask **Nickole Evans** of Kennewick, Washington, the same question, prepare to get a *list*.

Evans is a community activist and organizer, a Girl Scout leader, an anti-violence crusader, a dispute resolution mediator and a National Youth Council board member. Her website, *www.y2kyouth.org*, covers issues such as child abuse, over-population, race relations and religion, and proposes solutions.

Her slogan is, "It takes but one child to educate a whole village. How one person can make a difference!" The website gives kids ideas on ways they can do that.

Evans walks her talk. She's organized a Brownie troop to assemble homework-helper packets for students from migrant families; explained the juvenile justice system to at-risk youth; trained low-income families, at-risk youth and the disabled in how to use information technology; advocated for children's literacy and for the humane treatment of animals; and helped start her region's first chapter of S.A.V.E. (Students Against Violence Everywhere.)

But Evans has more than her time and energy on the line; she's also risked her own safety. The Kennewick area has become home to refugees from various war-torn regions of the world and many of the young people in these families have grown up seeing violent acts as a way to communicate. Evans and a friend were on the receiving end of that perception when they were shot by young Bosnian refugees armed with BB guns. Instead of retreating to safety, Evans embarked on a personal mission into the Bosnian community to talk directly with the youth and their parents about non-violent behavior and respect for people and property.

If you ask why she thinks individual kids can make changes in their communities, Nickole Evans lets you know that, "If you just start, and other people see what you're doing, they want to join, so it begins to grow. It just takes some guts to make that start, to begin the chain reaction."

Comprehension & reflection
How did the refugees in this story perceive their world? People often say that perception creates reality. What does this mean? Did the refugees in this story create a violent reality to match their perception of the world? How would you say Nickole Evans perceives the world? How is she creating reality around *her* perception?

Nickole believes that one person's actions cause others to take action. Do you think she's right? If you've seen this happen, describe the event and the outcome.

Vocabulary

Find any words in this story that are not completely familiar to you. See if you can understand their meanings by the way they're used in the story. Then look them up in a dictionary and put them in your vocabulary notebook, with a brief definition of each one. Use each word in a sentence that you make up yourself.

"Walk" and "talk" are familiar words to everyone. What does it mean to put them together in the expression "she walks her talk"?

"Chain reaction" is a term from science, describing what happens when atoms are split. Talk to a science teacher about the process of a chain reaction. Nickole uses the term in a sentence about the actions of people, not atoms. Make up your own sentence about people, applying this term to their interactions.

If you put the prefix mis- on the word "perception," what happens to the meaning of the word?

Project possibilities

Nickole Evans is described as a "community activist and organizer." Interview five people in your school or community and ask them who they see as fitting that description. Ask them for details about the activities of each person they name.

Go to Nickole's website *www.y2kyouth.org* and see if any of her ideas for projects appeal to you.

If you were going to create your own website, would it include information about issues and problems that concern you? If so, what would those issues or problems be?

Protecting An Endangered Species: Humanity

We're losing the struggle to save endangered species. According to experts, only 3% of species alive 100 years ago still exist today. Others are becoming extinct at a rate of at least two each day. Victims include the Calabash tomato, Howling Mob sweet corn and Rat's Tail radishes, because this is an endangered list of plants.

Today the world depends on just 20 species of plants for 90% of its food. Three crops (corn, rice, and wheat) account for half of what the people of the world eat. As an example of what is gone, 86% of the varieties of apples people ate in 1900 are no longer grown.

Kent and Diane Whealy of Decorah, Iowa, were so concerned about these disappearing food crops that they started the Seed Savers Exchange to get more people saving and swapping the seeds for traditional fruits and vegetables.

If you've never eaten a Calabash tomato or a Rat's Tail radish, that might not seem important, but listen to the Whealys and you may change your mind.

They explain that throughout the thousands of years of agricultural history all over the world, people have grown foods, and they've always saved seeds from each crop so they can plant the next crop. In recent years, something new has happened—seeds and food have become big business.

Farmers now buy most of their seeds from giant petrochemical firms that have bought out small, independent seed companies and then eliminated thousands of varieties of seeds. It's simpler and more profitable to sell the seeds for just a few crops. And farmers are buying seed not just once but every year, because these commercial crops are hybrids—their seeds can't be used to grow new plants!

It's an expensive way for farms to operate. The commercial seeds are susceptible to pests and diseases, so farmers have to go back to the petrochemical companies to buy chemicals to kill the pests and diseases. It's also, the Whealys will tell you, dangerous to the world's food supply.

This is "a tale of greed, shortsightedness, and good intentions that have led to disastrous consequences," says Kent Whealy.

The Whealys say it's disastrous, not just because many of the now missing fruits and vegetables tasted wonderful, but also because a seed's genes tell a plant how to endure frosts and droughts, and how to resist pests and diseases. When old species become extinct, the survival secrets in their genes are lost forever. The few remaining varieties could all be wiped out by climate change, disease or pests. Global wipeout of these vulnerable crops could cause widespread famine.

That almost happened in 1970 when a major crop, corn, was being killed world-wide by a fungus. Fortunately, a rare heirloom variety of corn was found that resisted the fungus. The life-saving seed was not the property of a company; it had been preserved for 900 years by an Indian tribe!

The Whealys are on a mission to save the seeds our ancestors grew, and to keep the food supply strong and safe. They began in 1976 when they received a wedding gift from Diane's grandfather—heirloom seeds from his family's farm in Bavaria. Realizing how precious this gift was, they started a simple newsletter for people who might want to trade, grow and preserve heirloom seeds. At the end of the first year, they had just six subscribers; a year later, only 29. Nevertheless, the Whealys quit their jobs to work full time on the Exchange. They skated on the edge financially for years, but they never quit.

Now they've grown the Exchange into a network of thousands of members preserving over 20,000 varieties of fruits and vegetables. On their own land the Whealys grow over a thousand rare species, preserving hundreds of varieties of potatoes, peas, beans, lettuce and peppers. One species of bean they grow is descended from seeds that came to this country on the Mayflower! They also preserve traditional crops of Native Americans.

"We are the stewards of this sacred wealth and it's up to us to preserve and pass it on," says Kent Whealy. "That's why we're willing to dedicate our lives to saving as much as possible of this vanishing heritage."

It could be that the next time a global crop is threatened, the savior seeds will be found because one couple in Decorah, Iowa, saw a serious problem and stuck their necks out to do something about it.

To do

Comprehension & reflection

Had you ever heard of heirloom seeds before reading this story? Few people know about this issue of the world food supply being vulnerable.

Many people eat very few kinds of foods, by choice. If you're one of them, it may not seem important to you that there are hundreds of types of potatoes but only a few kinds in grocery stores. But what if the one variety you like were wiped out by a bug or by a plant disease? What if the rice that so many nations eat as their basic food were all killed in the fields? Consider then the importance of preserving plants that are disease- and pest-resistant. How would you rank the importance of this work compared to other problems of concern?

If only 3% of the students in your class were still there, how many people would be in the room? Pretty quiet, isn't it? When there are famines, first food disappears, then people. It can be argued that the Whealys' work is vital for preserving *our* species.

Vocabulary

Find any words in this story that are not completely familiar to you. See if you can understand their meanings by the way they're used in the story. Then look them up in a dictionary and put them in your vocabulary notebook, with a brief definition of each one. Use each word in a sentence that you make up yourself.

The story describes our food varieties as vulnerable and vanishing. Can you think of other words to continue the alliterations?

Find all the words in this story that are about "botany," the study of plants. Ask your science teacher to talk to you about their meanings and about the idea of saving heirloom seeds.

Project possibilities

If growing heirloom plants interests you, get some instructions from *www.seedsavers.org* on how to get started.

If you decide to grow some heirloom plants, are there people in your community who could really use the food you grow? And don't forget to let Seed Savers know what you're doing.

Small Person/Giant Spirit

When **Jason Crowe** was nine, he lost a beloved grandmother to cancer and announced that he was going to raise money for cancer research, "so that no one else should ever have to lose their grandma to cancer."

But Jason didn't save up chore money or lemonade-stand profits—he became a publisher. His monthly newspaper for kids, *The Informer*, grew to have subscribers in 29 states and 15 foreign countries, with the proceeds going to cancer research. Jason researches, writes and edits articles on conservation, non-violence, religious tolerance, racial unity, and animal rights, all with a viewpoint that kids can help make the world a better place. Jason's theme is "kid power."

Jason told his subscribers a story that he couldn't stop thinking about: the story of the Cellist of Sarajevo. During the siege of that city, 22 men, women and children standing in a line to buy bread were killed by a mortar shell. Cellist Vedran Smailovic saw it happen. For 22 days after the massacre, Smailovic, dressed in his concert tuxedo, sat in the mortar crater at the hour the people had died, and played his cello. Totally exposed to the snipers and the artillerymen who had killed so many innocent people, Smailovic sent beautiful music out of the crater, into the hostile air.

Jason determined to keep the story alive as a way to remind people that harmony was the antidote to war. He organized a cello concert at the University of Evansville to honor Smailovic; he organized a vigil and memorial service for the dead, inviting artists, writers and musicians to perform.

Then he had a bigger idea: if the French could send the Statue of Liberty to this country, we could send a statue of the cellist to Sarajevo. Jason enlisted authors, politicians, teachers, students, celebrities and a sculptor in his cause. He wrote a book about the courage of Bosnian children and about all the kids around the world who were trying to help them, all proceeds, of course, to help pay for the statue of The Cellist of Sarajevo.

In a letter asking his support for the statue project, Jason reminded the US President that he had said in his Inaugural speech, "Nothing big ever came from being small." "Even though I am small literally," Jason wrote, "I don't *think* small."

Organizer, humanitarian, peace activist, editor, publisher, researcher, writer Jason Crowe had just turned 11 when he wrote that perceptive description of himself.

To do

Comprehension & reflection

If you've ever put forward an idea for a project and asked adults to support that idea, did you find them to be encouraging and supportive, or disrespectful? Jason was often brushed off and even insulted by people who didn't believe a child could or should be doing such things. He says it's important to keep going until you find people who *will* assist you.

Consider the advantages and disadvantages of being very young when creating projects such as Jason's.

What idea did Jason want to communicate with the statue of the cellist? Think of other works of art that communicate the same message.

Vocabulary

Ask a teacher of music or art to give you three words that are important to understanding a piece of music or a work of art.

When people say someone is "small," they often mean that person is mean, unimportant, or of little value. See how many meanings you can find for this word.

Project possibilities

Go to *http://members.sigecom.net/jdc/* to find out what Jason's doing lately.

If you share Jason's belief in "kid power," think about ways you might use it as Jason does, to make the world a better place.

If you started a newspaper, what issues would it cover?

*Jim McCloskey,
on the right,
celebrating
with one of the
innocent men he
helped free.*

A Ministry Behind Bars

Between them, Jimmy Landano and Joyce Ann Brown spent more than 30 years in prison for crimes they didn't commit. They'd still be there if it hadn't been for **Jim McCloskey** (back row on the right), a man the *Los Angeles Times* has called "one of the nation's best detectives." He's probably the *only* one who's also an ordained minister.

Back when he was a successful businessman, McCloskey heard the call to the clergy. He abandoned his career to enter Princeton Divinity School. As part of his training, McCloskey counseled prison inmates, among them a lifer named Chiefie De Los Santos. After listening for months to De Los Santos's protestations that he'd been railroaded by a lying jailhouse witness, McCloskey finally promised to take time off from his studies and look into the case. After *three* years of hard work, McCloskey was able to prove not only that De Los Santos hadn't done the deed, but also that the prosecutor had known all along that the witness was lying.

McCloskey forced the state to reopen the case, and De Los Santos was freed. McCloskey was so charged up by this success that he founded "Centurion Ministries," named for the Roman centurion who said at Christ's crucifixion, "Surely this man is innocent." The ministry serves a unique congregation—people unjustly imprisoned.

McCloskey uses patience, perseverance, common sense and hard work to dig up sloppy casework, lying witnesses and suppressed evidence. He visits witnesses again and again until they open up and admit the truth. "They all *want* to tell the truth," he says. "I'm asking these people to do something I don't even know if I'd have the courage to do." He spends a lot of time with them, easing them into doing the right thing, time he says police and attorneys rarely invest.

Not every Centurion legal triumph has a happy ending. Some freed prisoners, like Landano and Brown, bounce back, finding good jobs and personal happiness. But a few clients, including De Los Santos, have returned to jail—though at least they were actually guilty of the later charges. McCloskey says, "Chiefie changed my life, but unfortunately I didn't change his."

Centurion Ministries was soon besieged with so many calls for help that they can only take cases in which innocent people are serving life terms or facing death sentences. And once he takes a case, he sticks with it until the end—his longest case took him five years. If, however, he becomes convinced at any point that the client is lying, he drops the case.

This ministry is a far cry from the suburban church McCloskey once seemed destined for. Instead of spending his time with pleasant parishioners, he's with convicted felons, with perjurers, and recalcitrant cops in dingy prisons, courthouses and evidence rooms across the country. Grants and donations for Centurion are always slim and sometimes non-existent; McCloskey has foregone a lot of paychecks. Yet Jim McCloskey is a happy man. "You have to enjoy it; to feel a special calling and have it fit your human peculiarities," he says. "This work fits mine like a hand in a glove."

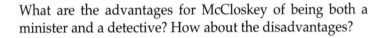

To do

Discussion & Reflection

Imagine what it feels like to champion an innocent prisoner and see that person proved innocent and released? On a scale of one to ten, how would you rate the personal satisfaction McCloskey earns from his work?

What are the advantages for McCloskey of being both a minister and a detective? How about the disadvantages?

Vocabulary

Do a little detective work of your own: find the origins of the term "to be railroaded." (Hint: good librarians love to help on this kind of search. And there's always the Internet.)

Make a list of words in the story that are related to the ministry. What does it mean to "have a calling"?

Make a list of the legal terms in the story.

Project possibilities

Go to *www.centurionministries.org* to get the latest on McCloskey's detective work.

What "peculiarities" do you have that might help you find a calling that fits you? In other words, what's unusual about your interests or abilities? If, for instance, you care a lot more about animals than your friends seem to, you might be called to start an animal shelter or to be a veterinarian. If justice and fair play are deeply important to you, you might be called to defend the innocent, as McCloskey does.

Are there any groups in your community that are already working on a problem you're "called" to take on? If there are, how might you assist them? If there aren't, could you get a project started to address the problem?

Sticking Up For Nobody Special

Eighth-grader **Sarah Swagart** knew an injustice when she saw one. Swagart was sure it was wrong for young skateboarders to be treated like criminals in her town of Oak Harbor, Washington. Kids who skated in her town's parking lots and on its sidewalks were threatened with fines of as much as $500 and 90 days in jail.

Not a skateboarder herself, Swagart could see that the skaters might be annoying, but they definitely didn't deserve treatment like that. The skaters were nobody special, she thought—just kids who needed a place to exercise their sometimes awesome skills.

Sarah's concerns prompted ideas for correcting the injustice. A picture began to form in her imagination of what could be done to create a legal place to skate. She formed an organization called "Nobody Special," whose goal was to get the skateboarders their own place to practice—and to get the community to recognize them as athletes, not hoodlums.

Swagart shared her vision with a local architect, who volunteered to design a skateboard park. But there had to be some place to put it. Sarah realized that no matter how much it scared her to speak in public, she had to start talking if the kids were going to get some land for their park.

She wrote up a petition for land and got signatures from kids, teachers, police officers, and even some store owners. Leading a delegation of 40 kids, she stood before the City Council and pointed out that the town had baseball fields, basketball courts, a roller rink and a swimming pool where kids could do those sports. What would be so different about accommodating the skateboarders?

The biggest problem, besides the kids' bad image, was insurance liability. What if a skater got hurt and sued the city? Swagart and the skateboarders got information on safety and liability from other towns that had skateboard parks. The City Council finally agreed there could be a skateboard park next to the public swimming pool.

The vision Sarah and the skateboarders had for their park caught on: they got a commitment from the SeaBees at nearby Whidbey Naval Air Station to do the construction work. Local businesses agreed to donate materials. And the kids organized a series of events to raise the money needed.

Sarah Swagart's vision of a skaters' park is now a reality. "Before this project I'd never stand up to anybody," she says. "Now, I would definitely encourage people to go for what they believe in."

Comprehension & reflection

When all the adults in a community seem to share a viewpoint, it can be awfully hard to change their minds, especially if you're a kid. How hard would it be for a shy person like Sarah to stand up and get an entire town to change its mind?

As in many other stories in this book, there is a stereotype at work in this story. The   skateboarders who were so "annoying" to the adults in the community were misperceived as criminals. Sarah's efforts not only got the adults to see the skateboarders as athletes, it also moved them off the streets and parking lots so they weren't irritating adults any more.

Vocabulary

Choose two words from this story and use a thesaurus to find other words that might be used instead. For example, find other words for deserve, definitely, awesome, hoodlums, or commitment.

"Skateboarder" is a word invented for a new sport. What other words can you think of that have been invented for an activity or invention that didn't exist 20 years ago? (Hint: there are hundreds in sports and in technology.)

Project possibilities

Are there people who are looked at negatively and unjustly by your community or your classmates? What could you do to help the community or your class see them as they really are?

Are there enough places for kids to exercise and play sports in your community? If there aren't, how could you start solving that problem?

The Safety Inspector

"If you think you'll make a difference here, you're kidding yourself. Nobody makes a difference here." That warning came from a coworker who was welcoming **Casey Ruud** to his first day as a safety inspector at the Hanford Nuclear Reservation in Washington State.

Ruud took his assignment seriously, knowing that Hanford was using uranium and plutonium to make detonators for nuclear weapons. Accidents with these deadly materials could poison groundwater and farmland for centuries. If any uranium and plutonium were stolen, it could be used by this nation's enemies to make weapons. Safety was clearly a vitally important job at Hanford.

Hanford was built during WW II so the buildings and equipment were aging. Ruud found dozens of cracks in equipment welds, every one of them dangerous. He reported them all to the plant's management so they could be repaired. He examined the equipment that plant workers used to make the nuclear detonators. The people making detonators wore hoods and heavy gloves that fit into a protective box so the workers were shielded from radiation. Ruud found that the filter on one box was filled with plutonium so the box was no longer safe to use. He reported this danger immediately, with his strong recommendation that production be stopped so the filter could be cleaned. Instead of stopping production to clean the filter, the plant manager slammed Ruud's report down on a table and stormed out of the room.

Shutting down production would be costly to the company, so the manager refused to order a cleanup. Workers were ordered to just yank the plutonium-clogged filters out by force, their hands covered only by rubber gloves. Twice, workers following this order were cut and deadly plutonium entered the cuts. Because employees were injured, the plant managers had to make a report on the incidents. Their report blamed the workers for not following proper safety procedures.

Ruud knew from his own investigation that it wasn't the workers' fault. He could also see that none of the safety problems he was reporting were being fixed. He found drums of plutonium just sitting in a hallway. Nearby, a child's toy wagon was full of nuclear detonators. He uncovered falsified records about a shipment of plutonium that was supposed to be accounted for, and spoke with a frantic worker who had lost track of four 55-gallon drums of plutonium.

An engineer at the plant anonymously sent Ruud a book of flawed designs within the plant, confirming his suspicions that there were even more safety problems than he had found on his own. Ruud reported to his supervisors that Hanford was vulnerable to thefts by terrorists, to deadly fires and to catastrophic explosions. Still, nothing changed.

Thousands of miles away, NASA's space shuttle Challenger blew up, killing its entire crew. Ruud learned that some of the managers at Hanford had also worked on the Challenger, and that they had ignored warnings of a possible explosion and refused to relay the warnings to NASA. Ruud realized that the same people were behaving the same way at Hanford.

Ruud's criticisms were getting noticed even though nothing was changing. The company's contract to run the site, a job worth $4 billion, was at stake and instead of fixing the safety violations, Hanford managers pressured him to keep quiet. If he was "a good company man," they told him, "he'd be well taken care of."

But Ruud was dedicated to safety, not to a company or to his own career advancement. Ruud took the next step. He "blew the whistle" by speaking to the *Seattle Times*, which ran a long and alarming story on the problems at Hanford. Ruud was called to testify before Congress, the Hanford plant was shut down, and a new company was brought in to manage the site.

Ruud had done the right thing, but he was a marked man. The new Hanford managers fired him almost immediately. One of them told him this was simply what happened to people who testify before Congress. Some residents of his community feared that Ruud's disclosures would close Hanford forever, causing massive job losses. They ostracized him. Some parents told their kids not to associate with his kids. "Nobody would even sit next to us at basketball games," Ruud remembers. A pastor called Ruud "evil" and directed his congregation not to patronize the frozen yogurt shop that Ruud was running to support his family. The shop went out of business.

Ruud moved to South Carolina when he finally landed a job at another nuclear facility. But within a few months, a manager from Hanford recognized him and got him fired again. This time, he was escorted out of the plant by guards with machine guns. A colleague there told Ruud, "I'm surprised they haven't killed you."

Ruud's dedication to public safety had enraged his employers but it attracted the United States Environmental Protection Agency, which sent him back to Hanford as a *federal* safety inspector, one who could not be fired by the plant's managers. He went back to work, finding safety hazards and helping design a massive cleanup of the heavily toxic site.

He was still the most unpopular person in the community, and he still had to struggle against the managers' unwillingness to change, but the safety of people and the environment was at stake, now and thousands of years into the future.

"Sure it was hard," Ruud will tell you. "But it had to be done. When things got really tough, I did think of chickening out. But then I'd think, I'm a Giraffe. I've got to keep sticking my neck out. And I'd go on."

A member of the Hanford Advisory Board said at the time, "There's a lot of bad decisions that never get made because they're afraid they're going to hear about it from Casey."

Today Ruud is proud that attitudes toward whistle blowers, worker safety and the environment are improving, and that Hanford has changed. "The risk of a catastrophic accident at Hanford is minuscule now compared to what it used to be," says Casey Ruud, a villain to some, but a hero to many, many others.

To do

Comprehension & reflection

Having a job and supporting a family are good things; protecting the safety of all is a good thing. When institutions or businesses are asked to stop practices that threaten public safety, they often respond that making the requested changes would cost jobs. Using the Internet or the library, learn more about this ongoing tug-of-war between businesses and advocates of public safety. Where do representatives of labor, government, business and the environment stand on this issue? Who do you think is right? Why?

What would you have done if you'd been in Casey Ruud's shoes? Why?

Have you ever been in a situation in which everyone around you had one opinion and you held another? If you have, what did you do? How hard is it to be the only one who has a different opinion?

Vocabulary

On a scale from one to ten, with one representing low risk and ten representing high risk, what number would you assign to a minuscule risk?

Other stories in this book take place on reservations for native Americans. Reservations are "reserved" for them. The word also implies that other people are restricted from entering. What reasons might there be for calling a nuclear production facility a reservation?

Project possibilities

If there's an important project in your community that's being done by one person who could use some support, how could you help?

A Continent of Children

Chellie Kew—photographer, wife, mother, holistic health practitioner, and former fashion model—had a dream: she would do a book of photographs of children touched by AIDS, focusing on their courage, not on the disease. Little did this American know that the dream would lead her to criss-cross sub-Saharan Africa, face danger and even death, and found a non-profit organization to help AIDS orphans on that continent.

When Kew's husband was transferred to Johannesburg, the couple and their teenaged children left their Oregon home, off on a two-year adventure. Soon Kew was learning first-hand about the devastating effects AIDS is having on the children of Africa.

Over several years, Kew traveled to squatters' camps, refugee villages and homeless shelters. She was amassing knowledge—and photographs—of the orphans of the AIDS scourge. "Entire villages are run by children," she reports. "All the adults are dead from the virus."

Kew started The "Q" Fund for AIDS, a non-profit dedicated to helping shelter, feed, protect and educate these orphans. To fund these projects, she planned to create a book of the photographs she'd been taking, sometimes in areas dangerous enough to require the "chaperone" services of an ex-CIA operative.

On one of her journeys, alone and hurrying to meet a missionary guide in Namibia, Kew swerved to avoid an impala. Her truck flipped on the washed-out road. When she came to, she realized she was hurt, far from the main road, and in leopard country. Then, a harrowing night and the morning horror of seeing leopard tracks around the wreck. The temperature in the truck would soon hit 120, and Kew needed medical attention. She started walking, hoping to find help, hoping to avoid attack by the predator tracking her. She told herself that she had to survive if she was to get the children's pictures to the world. After five hours of suffering and fear, she was found by a hunter.

"Terror, hunger, thirst, despair. Perhaps I needed the accident to fully comprehend the daily tragedies and triumphs these children face," she says now.

Kew is getting the children's pictures to the world in *African Journal, A Child's Continent*. With proceeds from the book and a few donations—over $40,000 so far—the "Q" Fund is building a community school in Zambia for 500 AIDS orphans, widows and the underprivileged. The Fund is also supporting a Soweto orphanage and AIDS education in Durban. Kew speaks extensively in the United States, talking about AIDS in Africa and promoting the book. She's organized a climb of Mt. Kilimanjaro by girls and women from around the world—the climbers will raise money the "Q" Fund will use to build another school for AIDS orphans.

Chellie Kew has realized her long-ago dream. She took the photographs, wrote the book, showed the courage of the children. And the dream turned out to be bigger and more rewarding than she could ever have imagined. "People say to me, 'Look what you're doing for these children in Africa.' But what they don't realize is what these children are doing for me."

To do

Comprehension & reflection

Imagine you're Chellie Kew. You've got your camera and you've got your dream: a book that will show the world the children who have lost their parents in the spread of AIDS across Africa. You're walking that road in Namibia, alone, injured, scared. What keeps you going?

OK now you're yourself, but you're living in a place where all the adults have died. You and the other kids your age are responsible for taking care of the younger children, making sure everyone is safe and healthy. What is your life like?

On a map, find Namibia, Zambia, Durban, Johannesburg and Mount Kilimanjaro. What are the relative sizes of the African continent and the North American?

People who work on behalf of others often say they get more from the work than they give. What does Kew mean when she talks about "what the children are doing for me"?

Vocabulary

In this story the word "chaperone" doesn't mean what it usually means, so the writer put it in quotes. This is a way to signal the reader that the unusual usage is intentional. How is the word usually used?

The prefix "sub-" means "below." What part of the map of Africa is sub-Saharan?

The word "predators" doesn't always mean animals. In history, in the news, in books you've read, are there *people* you might call predators?

Project possibilities
Check out *www.qfund4aids.org* to see what Chellie Kew is doing now.

Climbing a mountain to raise money is pretty unusual, but many people raise money for causes with walkathons, marathons, or bicycle races. Look into how these activities are organized to earn money.

Are there programs in your community to assist children whose parents have died? Is there any way you can assist these children?

Doing Business— the Right Way

To the guys he had hung with on Baltimore streets, **Charles Spann** looked like a fool. He'd been a big man—on his block—doing "business" deals, making fists full of money, as a dealer.

Then Spann's early "success" earned him time in a correction center, where he spent two years thinking only of getting back to the streets. But one staff member there saw strength and spirit in Spann and got the teenager into a rehab program called Fresh Start. There, Spann did a turnaround that brought him a lot of flak from lifelong friends.

When Spann went home from the program, he went into business again—a *legitimate* business called Tico Enterprises. Tico made wood products at the same time that it helped former gang members and drug dealers use their brains and skills in a positive way. The name came from a children's book about a small bird named Tico that helped people in need by giving them its own golden feathers.

Tico Enterprises made wood products from recycled materials and sold them to companies such as The Body Shop. They also restored boats and built docks. Half of Tico's profits went to Fresh Start, the organization that helped Spann turn his life around. Fresh Start used the contributions from Tico to help more young people in trouble.

Charles Spann's strength and spirit helped him become president of Tico Enterprises. In his new life as a big man at Tico, Spann learned to deal with bankers, retailers and media. He had to line up investments, make sales and do publicity for the company's "environmentally and socially benevolent" wood products He had to learn business, communications, and management skills. None of that was easy for a guy who hated school.

The alternative, he pointed out, isn't easy either—dying on cement, with a chalk line around your body. "I hate to hear about young black guys getting killed," Spann said. "They just say before the end of the news 'It was suspected to be drug-related.'"

Far from that perilous cement, Spann has found himself in the White House when the President honored Tico as a model program for the nation.

Charles Spann will tell you that all the challenges of his new life have been worth meeting, and that the best part has been showing kids who are still doing deals on street corners that there's a better way to get along in the world, a way that doesn't end in a chalk line on the sidewalk.

To do

Comprehension & reflection

Why would Charles Spann's turnaround bring him flak from his lifelong friends? How important to you are your friends' opinions? Would you say they influence your decisions and actions? Do *your* opinions influence other people's decisions and actions? Why or why not?

The story of Azim Khamisa and Ples Felix (page 67) brings up the concept of restorative justice. What connections can you see between Fresh Start and restorative justice?

Vocabulary

When writers put quotation marks around words, it can be to let the reader know that the words are used ironically. We all do this in speaking, by the tone of our voices or by our expressions—if we say "Right," with a particular inflection and facial expression, people know we really mean "Wrong." What does this writer mean by saying that Spann was a "business" "success" when he was younger?

Project possibilities

Is the overall attitude of your friends or acquaintances constructive or destructive? If you see it as destructive, what might you do to change that?

If you created an "environmentally and socially benevolent" business, what would it be? If the company gave part of its profits to a good cause, what cause would you choose and why?